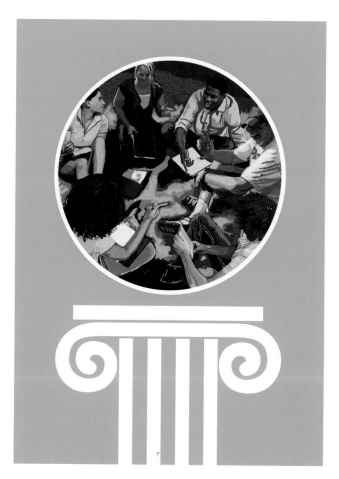

THE LONG-TERM
IMPACT
OF LEARNING TO
DELIBERATE

A Follow-up Study of Democracy
Fellows and a Class Cohort

Katy Harriger, Jill McI
Christy Buchanan, and Step

D1362339

Wake Forest University

The Long-Term Impact of Learning to Deliberate is published by Kettering Foundation Press. The interpretations and conclusions contained in this book represent the views of the authors. They do not necessarily reflect the views of the Charles F. Kettering Foundation, its directors, or its officers.

For information about permission to reproduce selections from this book, write to:
Permissions
Kettering Foundation Press
200 Commons Road
Dayton, Ohio 45459

This book is printed on acid-free paper.

First edition, 2016

Manufactured in the United States of America
ISBN: 978-1-945577-04-8

CONTENTS

INTRODUCTION 1

MILLENNIALS, POLITICS, AND DELIBERATION 7

MEASURING THE IMPACT
OF DELIBERATION 13

THE DEMOCRACY FELLOWS: RECOLLECTIONS
AND CONNECTIONS 14

CITIZENSHIP DEFINED 18

THE EFFECTS OF DELIBERATIVE DIALOGUE
ON COGNITIVE COMPLEXITY 23

CITIZENSHIP PRACTICED 28

POLITICS REASSESSED 41

EDUCATING FOR CITIZENSHIP 48

ANALYSIS OF THE SURVEY DATA 51

IMPLICATIONS FOR HIGHER EDUCATION 55

REFERENCES 57

APPENDIX A: METHODOLOGY 61

APPENDIX B: THE INTERVIEW INSTRUMENT 68

APPENDIX C: THE SURVEY INSTRUMENT 72

INTRODUCTION

This project had its genesis in the year 2000, with a question and a potential answer. The question was, what might institutions of higher education do to address young people's apparent disenchantment and disengagement with the political process? The potential answer was that if students learned to talk about politics in a different way, one less politically polarizing and more focused on finding solutions to the difficult policy problems that face us, they might be more willing to be engaged in the political process. We asked, if students learn to engage in deliberative dialogue, would they be able to imagine a different politics, one that they would want to be part of? At the end of the first stage of this project (2001-2005), we found that learning to deliberate did have a marked impact on students' attitudes about citizenship and their willingness to be engaged in the political process (Harriger and McMillan 2007). In this follow-up alumni study conducted in 2014-2015, we found that the impact of learning to deliberate was long-lasting. This monograph reports these findings.

A Different Way of Talking about Politics

The deliberation method used and evaluated in this study meets Gastil's (2008) definition of group dialogue, in which participants "carefully examine a problem and arrive at a well-reasoned solution after a period of inclusive, respectful consideration of diverse points of view." Our students at Wake Forest University were taught the method of deliberation used in the National Issues Forums (NIF), which includes considering multiple perspectives, surfacing and articulating competing values, identifying tensions and trade-offs, and looking for common ground for action (Mathews and McAfee 2003). Participants engage with a common text, called an issue guide, which offers three or more different perspectives on a policy issue. They talk with each other in a moderated dialogue that gives each perspective serious consideration and ends with a discussion that focuses on where participants find common ground that might lead to actionable ideas for change.

The first phase of the study involved a four-year program called Democracy Fellows. Thirty students were selected from the entering class to participate in the program. The selection process involved an application that included questions about their high school activities, as well as their attitudes toward citizenship and its responsibilities and the political process. We chose a group that reflected both the demographic diversity of the entering class and a diverse set of attitudes and experiences. When compared to a randomly selected group of students in the entering class, they were very much alike.

For the next four years, the Democracy Fellows (DFs) were exposed to the process of deliberative dialogue both inside and outside of the classroom. They started with a first-year seminar entitled "Democracy and Deliberation," in which they learned both the theory and practice of deliberation. They read political and communication theory and they engaged in three deliberative dialogues around public issues, each moderated by the professors. At the end of the semester, they identified a campus issue they felt needed attention and began the process of framing the issue for deliberation. During the second semester of their first year, they completed an issue guide, which focused on building community at Wake Forest. In their sophomore year, students were trained to moderate a deliberation and they organized and conducted the deliberation on campus. During their junior year, participants followed a similar process, but this time with a deliberation planned and conducted for the larger community of Winston-Salem, North Carolina. They first held a "listening session" with community leaders on challenges facing the community, and then adapted an NIF issue guide on urban sprawl, making the facts specific to Winston-Salem. They organized and moderated the deliberation on this issue off campus, with members of the community as participants. In their senior year, the students were given opportunities to moderate dialogues sponsored by other organizations on campus and in the community. After each deliberative intervention, we conducted focus groups with the Democracy Fellows and a representative class cohort (our control group whose members will be referred to in this report as CCs) to assess the impact of the intervention.

This report focuses on an alumni study of the Democracy Fellows 10 years after their graduation. They were again matched with a class cohort for the purposes of comparison, and all participants were interviewed and completed an online survey concerning their attitudes about, and involvement in, civic engagement. After a preview of our key findings, the report details the justification, methods, and results of the follow-up study. It concludes with a discussion of the implications of our findings for higher education institutions that seek to prepare citizens for engagement in their democracy.

A Summary of Findings

This study compares two very similarly situated groups (with the same under-graduate institution and a nearly identical distribution of majors, gender, and race/ethnicity). One group had the additional experience of having spent four years in the intensive study and practice of deliberative dialogue. The similarity of the two groups allows us to draw conclusions about the impact of that exposure to deliberation and to make some broader generalizations about the group as a whole. Here, we summarize our findings about how the groups were alike and how they were different.

Similarities of the Two Study Groups

Despite their different college experiences with deliberation, there were a number of ways the two groups show no significant difference as young adults. They are all voters, for example. They share a dislike for the nation's polarized political climate and the influence of money in politics. Their references to polarization were frequent; they present polarization as pervasive, and say that it inhibits their willingness, and sometimes ability, to engage in political discourse. We were struck by the way that, for both of these groups, the highly polarized environment seems to have made the workplace an arena in which political dis-cussion is particularly to be avoided, either because there are formal rules against it or an implicit understanding that disagreements of this type could have negative consequences for their ability to do their jobs.

They all value service to their community and they give their university credit for encouraging them to serve. They recognize that their academic experiences prepared them well and they share a belief in their ability to use their voices to be heard about matters they care about. Although Democracy Fellows are more willing than the class cohort to engage with people who have different points of view, all of the alumni prefer political conversations with people whom they trust.

These alumni have a shared perception of their ability to effect change in their communities, in their workplaces, and in the political arena. They feel most competent in the community setting, especially if they work with others, and least efficacious in making change in national politics. The workplace is a mixed bag, with their sense of efficacy depending on their position in the organization, its size, and whether it is a political job. Not surprisingly, those with jobs in the political and policy realm feel more politically efficacious than those who work elsewhere.

Neither group has had much opportunity to engage in structured dialogue, but for those who have, their primary motivation for engaging in these activities is their desire to know more about an issue that they care about.

Finally, after almost a decade in the "real world," these young adults have both positive and negative things to say about how their post-college experiences compare to their college life. On the one hand, they believe that having more experience and knowledge, and being more "settled" in a community, makes them more powerful and more engaged than they were when they were encased in the "bubble" of campus life. On the other hand, they have become less idealistic about the possibility of change.

Distinctive Differences of Democracy Fellows

The Democracy Fellows' reflections on their experience with deliberation are almost uniformly positive. Even those few who had some less than glowing comments nonetheless recognized that they had gained skills from the program that they continue to use and value. For both personal and practical reasons, they recommend the longitudinal nature of the program. They recall both the philosophical underpinnings of deliberation, as well as the particular practices they learned in the program, and they continue to apply these skills in their daily lives 10 years after graduation. For them, the Democracy Fellows program was the most significant preparation they received for their civic and political lives.

The majority of DFs have a complex and nuanced understanding of citizenship and its responsibilities. They see it as multidimensional, involving both political participation and a sense of identity or connection to a political community and its values. Similarly, their understanding of the political process and how it works is more sophisticated. When asked what they would change about politics as it is practiced, they are more likely than members of the class cohort to emphasize the connection between structural components of the system and the things they dislike about politics—especially polarization and the role of money.

Throughout their interview responses, the DFs show a higher level of sensitivity to, and awareness of, the extent to which context matters, and how the communities within which they operate shape their participation, their efficacy, and their willingness or ability to speak their minds and engage with others in political conversation. They also place greater value on being informed than do members of the class cohort. DFs often expressed a belief that knowledge provides the power that will have an impact on whether they can make a difference in their communities and in their workplaces.

Many of the Democracy Fellows continue to be involved in politics. More of them have jobs in the political and policy arenas than do the CCs; more are likely to engage in activities like working on campaigns and giving money to candidates; and more are likely to say that public service is honorable and that they can imagine themselves in that role. Given the literature cited later in this report, which finds that millennials have relatively low levels of political and civic engagement, low levels of confidence in government, and low levels of political knowledge, our data suggest that the Democracy Fellows are different, not just from their class cohort, but from their generational cohort as well.

Finally, the DFs' political communication profile can be described as more elaborated, nuanced, curious, and bold than that of the class cohort. Most of their interview responses were longer and more complex than those of their cohort, reflecting the deliberative consideration of various sides of an issue and their interrelationship. They expressed a great deal of interest in the points of view of people who think differently than they do, and this influences how they pursue the political knowledge that they value. Despite their dislike for the polarized climate they find themselves in, they were more likely than members of their class cohort to express a sort of communicative fearlessness. DF responses revealed that they are more eager to engage with people who hold different beliefs, but they want to do it in contexts of reasonable, open-minded exchange.

Distinctive Differences of the Class Cohort

Our comparison group differed from the Democracy Fellows not only in their lack of exposure to deliberation, but also in a number of other important ways. When asked about what college experience was most important in preparing them for their civic and political life, they were far more likely than the Democracy Fellows to mention community-service experiences through their various organizational attachments, particularly Greek life. They were also more critical of their academic experience as a means of preparation, characterizing it as too abstract and removed from the "real world" they have encountered.

The CCs' conceptions of citizenship were more legalistic and less complex than those of the Democracy Fellows. They also valued being informed more than being politically active, and there was a substantially larger number of cohort respondents whose only political activity is voting. Their engagement is more likely to be community service than political involvement, continuing the pattern formed during their college experiences and reflecting the literature on the characteristics of their generation.

When asked what they would change about the political system, their answers tended more toward what might be called "surface" solutions than the answers of DFs. For example, more of them seem to believe that if you just change the political actors you would get a different outcome. What is wrong with politics for many of them is the quality of political candidates, rather than something more structural, such as flawed policy or structural imbalance.

The political communication profile for the class cohort comes across in the interviews as quite different from that of the Democracy Fellows. More often than DFs, the CCs reported that they are likely to avoid conversations that they believe could harm important social relationships or breach social conventions, although some of them enjoy argumentative exchanges in certain contexts. If they seek political conversation, they are more likely than DFs to prefer doing it with people who will confirm their own views or with whom they feel safe and comfortable. Although they have found occasions and groups in which to engage in structured dialogue, their responses regarding the practice suggest that CCs find deliberation to be a less valuable use of their time, and often inconsistent with their personal interests, when compared to responses from DFs.

In the pages that follow, we flesh out these findings. Using extensive citations from the interviews, analysis of survey responses, and a measure of cognitive complexity, we demonstrate the enduring impact of learning to deliberate.

MILLENNIALS, POLITICS, AND DELIBERATION

This follow-up study brings together research insights from the literature on political socialization, political participation, and deliberative democracy, with a particular focus on whether and how interventions during the college experience might shape subsequent civic engagement. This research helped shape the four-year (2001-2005) longitudinal study of the Democracy Fellows program at Wake Forest University (Harriger and McMillan 2007) and informs the follow-up study, designed to discern whether the effects of the deliberative interventions during the college years are still present 10 years later.

Political Socialization and Generational Analysis

Political socialization is the process by which people come to hold the beliefs they do about politics and determine their role in the political process. Those who study political socialization are interested in how experiences in various social contexts shape people's perceptions, attitudes, beliefs, and behaviors in the political realm. Early political socialization work focused on childhood and adolescence, concluding that most of one's political socialization is determined in these early years, with family and education being the most significant influences (or "agents") in the process (Easton and Dennis 1969; Greenstein 1965; Jennings and Niemi 1974; Sigel and Hoskin 1981).

The initial assumptions that this "early learning would remain relevant for, and persist into, adulthood" (Sigel 1989) began to be challenged in the 1970s and 1980s by scholars studying the ways that experiences in early adulthood and other transitional stages in life could, and did, alter political worldviews. For example, panel studies of young adults in high school and college found that the early socialization that made the young so trusting of government could be disrupted by government scandal and misconduct. Reacting to the Vietnam War and the Watergate scandal, young adults in those years had a "startling drop in trust" in government compared to the views of previous generations. "This spectacular drop," writes Roberta Sigel, "cannot be attributed to maturation alone but rather is a vivid example of period effects as they interact with the aging process" (2-3).

There are three categories of explanations for why political socialization is ongoing and why adults are susceptible to political change. The first involves "societal phenomena," such as war, economic conditions, and rapid technological change. The second is what has been identified as "time lag" or "temporal aspects," which refer to the time gap "between when youthful learning about politics takes place and the assumption of 'real' political roles as citizens" (Steckenrider and Cutler 1989, 57). Finally, and particularly relevant to young adulthood, is the transition to new roles, such as college student, full-time employee, spouse, and parent. These new roles create "new role relationships, experiences, social environments, and political responsibilities and opportunities, any of which can lead to changed political outlooks" (58). Adult socialization happens during this time "not necessarily because an individual rejects the values and behavioral patterns learned in childhood but because they may be inadequate or irrelevant for the new or modified roles taken on as an adult. The adult either wants, or is forced, to learn new, different, or additional ways of thinking, feeling, and behaving politically to cope with the new demands accompanying the new role" (64-65).

Young adulthood, usually defined as the ages between 18 and 30, represents a period of time in which there is considerable potential for attitudes about politics to be disrupted or altered. During this time, young adults "chart a course for their future and 'take stock' of the values they live by and the kind of world they want to be part of. . . . Exploring alternative political perspectives, working with people from different social backgrounds, and wrestling with a range of perspectives on social issues provide opportunities to reflect on one's own views and decide where one stands" (Flanagan and Levine 2010, 160). In contrast to older adults, people in this age group have more "unsettled" lives "as they move into and out of institutional settings such as school and work." They have many opportunities for civic engagement during these times, although these tend to be "episodic." This period of time is critically important in predicting future involvement in politics, for "the political identities formed in the early adult years are highly predictive of the positions individuals will hold in middle and even late adulthood" (161).

Harriger and McMillan's 2007 study, which found that experiences in college could alter students' views about the political system and their role in it, has been confirmed by many other studies. A college education continues to be the most significant predictor of the likelihood that individuals will vote and participate more widely in the political process (Schlozman et al. 2012). Studies of the college experience during different political eras demonstrate that "the 'broadening' of the world of ideas and experience that new peers, facts, and concepts bring about suggests an opening or 'liberalizing' process" (Steckenrider and Cutler 1989, 69). But the tenor of the political times has an impact as well. A study from the 1930s found that college tended to make students more politically liberal, while "the same dynamic may well help explain the politically conservative atmosphere on college campuses in the 1980s." The key point is that the role transition to college student "serves to introduce contemporary broader social and historical themes to the student, i.e., what cohort analysts . . . refer to as *period effects*: liberalizing in a liberal period, conservatizing in a conservative period" (69).

Another significant role transition for young adults is from student to full-time employee. The world of work has the potential for profoundly affecting one's attitudes about politics. Steckenrider and Cutler (1989) argue that "role and role transitions associated with work are among the most significant sources of adult socialization, quite often with both indirect and direct political consequences. . . . The socialization that surrounds the role of wage earner is so central that it can shape the individual's political beliefs and ideology, habits and lifestyle, status in society, and even self-image" (70). There is evidence that the kind of work one does and the degree of control one has over his or her work environment can have significant effects on the degree of alienation or efficacy people feel. Evidence suggests that skills one learns in some jobs are easily transferable to the political realm (i.e., public speaking, writing, organizing meetings). Jobs in which people are included in the decision-making process tend to contribute to feelings of political efficacy. Work can be so tied up with one's identity that unemployment, especially for sustained periods of time, has been shown to have a significant negative impact on political participation (Buss and Hofstetter 1981).

Closely related to the study of political socialization is generational analysis that seeks to discover what generational cohorts have in common. This analysis is based on the fact that socialization takes place within a larger social context and that young people will be influenced by "period effects," including major events, such as war and economic depression (the "greatest generation"), and broader social changes, such as the widespread use of television (baby boomers) or the Internet. The millennial generation (born between 1985 and 2004), of which the Democracy Fellows and their cohort were in the vanguard, has been much analyzed.

As Peter Levine (2011) warns us, we should be cautious in making generalizations about a group as large, diverse, and amorphous as a generation. He notes that different analyses of the same generation have been both glowing (Greenberg and Weber 2008) and sharply critical (Bauerlein 2008). Nonetheless, Levine identifies "the most salient characteristics" of millennials as "fondness for online social networking, experience with volunteer service, comfort with diversity, unprecedentedly high levels of support for the winning presidential candidate [in] 2008, low interpersonal trust, low levels of formal group membership, and particularly wide economic disparities and divergence of experiences by social class" (Levine 2011, 4).

In general, most studies of millennials conclude that this generation is distinctive in its "propensity to serve (marked by record-high volunteering levels), appreciation of diversity, creativity, and entrepreneurship, and resistance to the dead-end ideological debates and culture wars of previous generations" (Levine 2011, 4). Survey data from 2006 on attitudes of young people in this generation suggest relatively low levels of political and civic engagement (with community service higher than other forms), low levels of confidence in government, and low levels of political knowledge. Confirming the findings of a number of studies, those data also show that this generation is more tolerant of difference than previous generations were. Finally, this study found the evidence, seen in recent electoral contests, that this generation leans more strongly Democratic than the generation that preceded it (Lopez et al. 2006).

A 2013 report notes that, with regard to the civic engagement of this generation, the glass is both half full and half empty. On the positive side, the report notes that 50 percent of voters between 18 and 29 turned out in the 2012 presidential election and clearly had an impact on its outcome because of their overwhelming support for President Obama. In addition, their rates of volunteering continue to be much higher than those of previous generations, as is their use of social media as a means of political engagement. On the other hand, it notes the degree to which the high turnout continues to exclude large numbers of young people in lower socioeconomic classes who lack college degrees. In addition, "conventional group membership, attendance at meetings, working with neighbors, trusting other people, reading the news, union membership, and religious participation are all down for young people since the 1970s" (CIRCLE 2013, 4).

In 2007, the Center for Information and Research in Civic Engagement (CIRCLE) released *Millennials Talk Politics*, a study that involved focus group and survey data from a broad range of college campuses across the nation. The study's authors recognized that close to half of young people between 18 and 25 were not in college, but noted that it is important to study college students because their "education often gives them access to leadership positions in major institutions in the United States and around the world" (CIRCLE 2013, 4). The CIRCLE study found attitudes about politics similar to those we discovered in our single-campus study. Millennials were more engaged, mostly through community service, than the previous "generation X" (whose alienation and disengagement from politics contributed to much of the revived attention to civic education in the 1990s). While not considered as alienated as their predecessors, millennials were more likely to be involved at the local level than with national politics. They had a great dislike for the polarization they saw, particularly at the national level, a distrust of the "spin" they recognized in most media coverage of politics, and a desire for more opportunities to have meaningful dialogue around public issues, a finding that was confirmed in the 2007 Wake Forest study. The report's authors recommended that students be given "the opportunities and space for deliberation on public issues" (Kiesa et al. 2007, 5).

The Impact of Deliberation

Attention to how to better educate students for their future roles as democratic citizens has increased significantly in the last decade. In 2012, the National Task Force on Civic Learning and Democratic Engagement released a "Call to Action," (National Task Force on Civic Learning and Democratic Engagement 2012) stressing the importance of taking seriously the role of higher education institutions in preparing students for civic life. The authors of the report noted that a survey of 2,400 college students in 2009 found that only one-third of the respondents felt "that their civic awareness had expanded in college, that the campus had helped them learn the skills needed to effectively change society for the better, or that their commitment to improve society had grown" (41). The report chronicled the many ways colleges and universities were responding to this call, and included discussion of dialogue and deliberation as one means that students could be taught citizenship skills and dispositions. In addition to Harriger and McMillan's 2007 study, the report noted research on the impact of intergroup dialogue projects (ASHE 2006; Gurin et al. 2011) and concluded that the research thus far suggests that deliberative dialogue is a high-impact methodology for preparing students for their civic roles (National Task Force 2012).

The impact of deliberation on attitudes and behavior has been studied now in multiple contexts, not just in academic settings (Dedrick et al. 2008; London 2010), but in communities across the country and around the world (Nabatchi 2010a, 2010b; Nabatchi et al. 2012; Neimeyer 2011). The degree to which interest in this approach has grown as a way of addressing the "democratic deficit" (Nabatchi 2010a) is reflected in the fact that the *Annual Review of Political Science* included an extensive essay reviewing the research on deliberation in 2004 (Delli Carpini et al. 2004) and two additional essays in 2008 about using empirical methods to study the impact of deliberation on participants (Mutz 2008; Thompson 2008). As another indicator of the extent to which there is broad scholarly interest in the subject, a new *Journal of Public Deliberation* has been established as a peer-reviewed outlet for research on deliberation.

The Need for Further Research

The current interest in the impact of civic education practices points to the need to assess what we know and what we don't know about what works to create "long-lasting habits of civic engagement" (Hollander and Burack 2009). In 2008, the Spencer Foundation, which focuses its philanthropic efforts on supporting educational research, brought together a group of scholars and practitioners in the area of civic engagement to discuss the state of the field. They were asked to think about what we already know and what we still need to know in order to establish a research agenda going forward. The conclusions most applicable to this study included (1) the need to identify "the academic and co-curricular elements that most impact student civic engagement and *long-term commitment* to civic engagement (emphasis added), and (2) the need for longitudinal approaches and data" (Hollander and Burack 2009, 6-8). Further, Levine (2011) notes that "the application of deliberative democracy to youth civic engagement has not been thoroughly explored"(5), but that the research thus far suggests that the relationship holds promise. In addition to Harriger and McMillan's 2007 study, reviews of the impact in the educational context suggest that the experience of deliberating has a positive impact on developing civic skills (Hess 2009). The purpose of our current study was to pursue these lines of research to see whether there were particularly effective strategies that our students recalled and retained over time, and whether there was any long-term impact of the deliberative interventions that our students were exposed to during their four years of college.

MEASURING THE IMPACT
OF DELIBERATION

The questions pursued in this follow-up study focus on the longer-term impact of the deliberative experiences that the Democracy Fellows had while in college. Do Democracy Fellows continue to differ from their peers in attitudes about politics and citizenship? Do they continue to use the lessons they learned in other aspects of their lives? If so, how? If not, why?

We studied two groups of alumni from Wake Forest. One was made up of alumni who had participated in our original four-year Democracy Fellows program and who had extensive exposure to deliberative theory and practice. We were able to locate 20 of the students from this group. The control group was comprised of alumni from the same class (2001-2005) who had not been exposed to the program. The control group was randomly selected from a list obtained from the alumni office. Rather than trying to locate the original cohort from the list provided to us, we closely "matched" the two groups in terms of race and ethnicity, gender, and major in college. All members of both groups participated in phone interviews of approximately one hour each and filled out online surveys.* They were all asked the same set of questions, except that, in the phone interviews, the Democracy Fellows were asked some additional questions about their experience in the program.

We employed three different approaches to analyzing the data: content analysis of the interviews, Integrative Complexity Scoring (ICS) on one set of the interview questions, and quantitative analysis of survey data. A more detailed explanation of the methodology and the steps followed to determine reliability and significance may be found in Appendix A.

---

* Responses to these queries, quoted throughout this report, were subject to editing for brevity and clarity.

THE DEMOCRACY FELLOWS: RECOLLECTIONS AND CONNECTIONS

Both groups of alumni were asked the same interview questions, but in order to bring out any particular recollections of the Democracy Fellows program, an additional three questions were asked only of the DFs at the end of the interviews:

- In reflecting back on your participation in the Democracy Fellows program, what stands out to you about that experience?

- Are you finding any use for your deliberative experience in your post-college, adult life?

- Are there other ways that the Democracy Fellows experience has influenced your behavior or choices?

To avoid the possibility that the DFs might feel obligated to make positive responses to Harriger and McMillan, all of the DF interviews were conducted by the two individuals on the research team who had had no previous association with the DFs or with the original project.

The strongest memories of the program were both personal and practical. They demonstrate that despite a decade of distance from the program, DFs had very clear memories of what they had learned and why it still mattered.

Many recalled sharing the life-changing experience of the terrorist attack of 9/11, as DFs were actually in their First-Year Seminar class when the twin towers fell. One DF recalled thinking that it was some "weird sci-fi clip" that the professors had devised for them to analyze. Another widely shared memory was the bond between the DFs, initiated in 2001 and solidified over the next four years. Many spoke of the "unique" experience of starting this program with a group of intimidated, overwhelmed first-year students "at a new school and in a new experience" and staying together until the end. More than one respondent talked of "growing up together."

Beyond the personal, however, was praise for the First-Year Seminar, its goal, and its enactment. One DF summarized it as taking a bunch of 18-year-olds and teaching them "how to talk to folks who don't have the same beliefs as they do." Another described it as "giving them a new way to think." Different aspects of the deliberative process itself were cited: even-handed presentation of an issue, the opportunity for expressing personal opinions, analyzing pros and cons, finding common ground, active listening, communication skills, and neutrality, among others. The logistics of deliberation intrigued others: selecting an issue for discussion, research, creating an issue guide, generating interest within the public, recruiting participants, advertising, and delivering the deliberation event itself; some were especially struck by the value of learning to moderate a discussion. Overshadowing all the aspects of the DF program that stood out for these alumni was the almost universal belief that they had learned to better respect the opinions and expressions of people who thought differently from themselves—or, as even one of the less enthusiastic DFs put it, "[I now think that] lots of viewpoints are valid."

Then and Now

In the original study, DFs identified all the ways they were putting their deliberative skills to use in their lives. We wanted to know whether they were still using those skills in their adult lives. In their responses, we were struck both by the breadth of the venues in which they reported using their skills and by the specificity with which they recalled the procedures and ways of thinking that they had learned. While appreciation for the wide utility of deliberative skills is consistent with our original findings, the graduates of the class of 2005 had not yet tested that utility in what they euphemistically called "the real world"—and now they have.

These respondents report utilizing deliberative training in law, medicine, religion, politics, teaching, community activism, and interpersonal relationships, including marriage. One DF, who presently leads a Yale University research team, summarized what we heard from many when she said, "I constantly use those skills in my daily job." She went on to say:

> I think that that was something . . . really valuable that I received.
> [Deliberation is] the name of what I do—it's interdisciplinary and
> it's collaborative. Every single day I have to work with people all over
> the US and all over the world who don't necessarily have the same
> viewpoint [as I do], who don't have the same training, and who don't
> have the same background. I think one of the reasons I've been able
> to be effective is because I learned a lot of those skills when I was 18.

Just as interesting is how well respondents recall the specific skills they were taught and offer specific examples of deliberation-in-practice in their particular professional settings:

We talked a lot about what voices weren't at the table and one of the things I think that's helpful for me as an adult . . . and having had that experience is . . . trying to really be cognizant, both in my professional life as well as in my community life, of who we aren't thinking of—who is not being included here. It's really helped me professionally.

I think I used college as a place to learn . . . how to have a political conversation . . . rather than taking a stand on something and not allowing myself to be influenced by anyone else. . . . I think [it] requires a lot of training to learn how to . . . find out where the people you're trying to talk to are and then take them with you on to more understanding. . . . We got those kinds of skills in training how to be a good moderator, how to set the ground rules of a conversation . . . how to listen . . . how to try to pull people out of their shells.

The DFs were asked to consider whether a causal link existed between their deliberative experience and the behaviors and life choices they have made. Some went there with no hesitation. One DF recounted that the community deliberation that he and his colleagues organized in 2004 on urban sprawl in the city of Winston-Salem had prompted him to adopt a minor in urban studies; another said that the Democracy Fellows program had inspired him to go to law school. Still another respondent said that she had come to college planning to study the natural sciences, but became interested in politics and policy because of the program. She now works in the area of environmental policy. Others were more cautious about drawing a direct causal link between specific personal decisions and the program they had experienced, but overwhelmingly, these adult DFs opined that they had become more open-minded, critical thinkers who had learned to speak and listen to others with empathy and respect, and that they continue to find deliberation philosophy and practices useful in myriad ways. Another strong outcome of the experience was that, as one DF put it, it "broadened my outlook on politics and improved my education as a citizen." Another DF, who described her upbringing in a "very conservative family and environment," learned that "it's okay . . . I don't have to vote as my parents vote. I think that the [DF] program gave me a sense of ownership over my political views."

There were a few DF respondents whose responses were not as positive. One remarked, "It [the Democracy Fellows program] started out too early for me. . . . I hadn't found myself at Wake." Another recalled that there were a few "very vocal individuals" in the First-Year Seminar class, and that "alternative viewpoints were not necessarily welcome." More than one DF lamented that, even though they remember the experience positively, they wish in hindsight that they had taken the program more seriously. Finally, one respondent, who had cited the values of the program in his life—critical-thinking skills, improved communication, and consideration of different viewpoints—concluded pessimistically that in politics today he fears there is not "a lot of room for the type of discourse [the program] teaches."

CITIZENSHIP DEFINED

The first set of questions we asked of respondents in both groups in our current study revolved around how they defined and practiced citizenship (see Appendix B). When they graduated from college in 2005, Democracy Fellows talked about citizenship and its responsibilities in language that differed from that employed by their class cohort. They were more likely to talk about working with others to solve problems in their community as opposed to engaging for the purpose of protecting their personal interests. In 2015, differences in conceptions of citizenship remained between the two study groups.

In developing codes for answers to this set of questions for the 2015 interviews, we focused on three possible conceptions of citizenship: *participatory*, *cultural/identity*, and *legal*. Participatory conceptions of citizenship focused on taking action, and included voting, running for office, staying informed, volunteering, helping others, joining the armed services, or being part of community groups. For example, responses coded as *participatory* reflected things such as:

> I think citizens should be active participants in their community. And that means, at the minimum, voting. But I've always felt [that] civic engagement is important. Volunteering, [and] helping out where you can, when you can, are part of being a good citizen.

> To be a citizen is to be an active [party in] the social contract. I guess I've come more and more [to the view] that we are all in this together. Right or wrong, good or bad . . . we owe it to each other to be active participants . . . be it in a conversational setting or simply by voting.

Cultural/identity conceptions focused on identifying with a culture, a place, or a set of values and experiencing a sense of belonging from them. It was characterized by talk of being part of a larger community or nation and the recognition that cultures and values varied from place to place. Exemplary statements coded under this category included, "I think, to me, being a citizen . . . means kind of having an identity in a country or nationality," and "I think a citizen is someone that is . . . a part of the fabric of a country. Usually, [you are a citizen] when you are born there, but there are certainly cases where you can apply to be a citizen of a country and I guess if you want to take on the values of [that] country, then you can become a citizen."

Legal citizenship conceptions were the most narrowly defined, and, as the name implies, focused on the legal requirements of citizenship. Thus, citizenship was what one had as a result of being born or naturalized in a particular place, or it was defined as obeying the law or meeting legal obligations. For example, one respondent defined citizenship by saying, "I guess just paying my taxes. And abide by the law," and another said, "I guess just being documented in the United States."

Figure 1 illustrates that there were differences between the DFs and CCs in terms of conceptions of citizenship and the responsibilities inherent in this concept. While a majority in each group identified both *participatory* and *cultural/ identity* aspects of citizenship, DFs were more likely than CCs to identify both as important. In the DF group, 19 of 20 DFs emphasized *participatory* aspects and 14 also emphasized *cultural/identity*. In the CC group, 16 of 20 discussed *participatory* aspects and 11 of the 20 identified with *cultural/identity*. A quarter of CCs, on the other hand, focused on *legal* definitions and responsibilities, while only 10 percent of DFs did so.

Figure 1: Comparisons of DFs and CCs in Conceptions of Citizenship

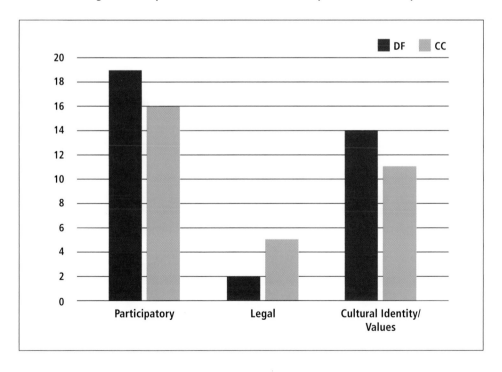

DFs who did give *legal* definitions of citizenship also mentioned *participatory* aspects of citizenship, while most of the CCs with *legal* definitions mentioned only the legal aspect of citizenship. For example, here is the statement of a DF coded both *legal* and *participatory*:

> I would say . . . as a citizen of a country you can't . . . violate established laws and regulations established to keep everybody safe. I would say also [that] your job as a citizen is to contribute and to be productive as part of society. . . . There are some people who choose to be free riders and don't give anything back, but I think that's one of the reasons why we have the tax system—so that you can also contribute to the country's sustainability.

In contrast, here is the statement of a CC coded only *legal*:

> I guess, we're born in this country and so basically that makes us citizens. So you have [the] basic rights of citizens . . . to vote [and to enjoy] the rights guaranteed by the Constitution.

Figure 2 demonstrates another difference that stood out between the two groups. DFs were twice as likely as CCs to emphasize the importance of staying informed, or being knowledgeable about what is going on in politics, as a responsibility of citizenship. This finding was consistent with survey results that

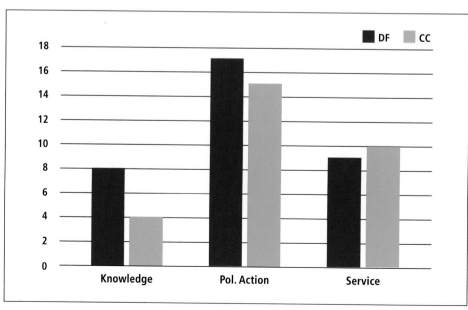

Figure 2: Comparison of DFs and CCs on Themes of Civic Responsibility

found DFs more likely to read a newspaper for information on politics and current events. DFs also often associated knowledge with participation. "I think that . . . probably the biggest obligation people have," said one DF, "is they need to be as informed as they are involved. Which means I think people shouldn't be voting because they've been told to vote a certain way. They should be voting because they've thought about it and read [about it]." Another said, "I think citizenship . . . requires active participation and knowledge . . . of the issues that are impacting the citizens, and active engagement as well as [the] desire to understand the community's needs and requirements."

In other ways the groups were quite similar. In each group, about half talked about the importance of service to one's community, something we would expect, given survey data that shows the importance that millennials place on community service, which we defined as volunteering or serving your community in some way other than through the political process. The following responses demonstrate the importance both groups placed on service:

> I guess a citizen . . . means being . . . an active part of your community and your society at large, caring for those around you, and caring for the greater good of the organization you're a part of, whether that's the US or . . . your local neighborhood or your city (CC).

> I think about . . . just how we help others in a community—things that we can do in order to build each other up and to provide assistance in times of need (CC).

> I think . . . there's an element of giving back to the community . . . in whatever manner you are able to, whether that's volunteering or financial donations. For me it tends to be more on the volunteering end (DF).

> I think that you should think about what's best for the community rather than just about your personal situation, which I think is something that often gets lost in the political scheme (DF).

DFs were slightly more likely than CCs to name political actions that should be part of citizenship (as the differences in the *participatory* category would suggest), but in both groups, a substantial majority named such acts. Notice, though, how DFs weave their talk about participation in politics with themes about knowledgeability and engaging with others:

> It's not just casting votes, it's also informing yourself [and] helping other people to better understand the issues at hand . . . so that everybody can be more informed and the outcomes can be better— more beneficial to everybody.

> From voting in yearly elections to . . . being aware of what's going on in your community or at a national or state level . . . I don't think you necessarily have to be out protesting in the streets or giving money to a political campaign or [advocating for] an issue. . . . In general, it's engagement with your community on issues that matter and engagement in the political process.

Many CCs also talked about political actions in terms of the responsibilities of citizenship, but as these examples show, with less connection to other citizenship themes:

> Participating in voting, participating in speaking out on injustice, or providing my opinion of things [in which] I want my feedback [to be] a part of the political process.

> I think to be a citizen, you need to be an active participant in the process of choosing the leaders that are going to represent you— whether that's voting or whether that's getting involved in various political action committees or just making your voice heard in some way.

THE EFFECTS OF DELIBERATIVE DIALOGUE ON COGNITIVE COMPLEXITY

We were able to probe more deeply into our graduates' perceptions of citizenship by using a method designed to assess an individual's critical reasoning pattern about a certain issue or construct. We hoped to learn the manner in which both alumni groups reasoned about citizenship and its responsibilities. Integrative Complexity Scoring (ICS) is a particularly useful methodology for assessing the impact of extensive exposure to the deliberative process. ICS measures the existence of two cognitive components:

- Differentiation, which entails the ability of the research subject to identify different dimensions of an issue and to recognize that there is more than one way to see an issue.

- Integration, which involves the ability to identify the relationships or interactions between those dimensions, and to recognize tensions and trade-offs.

The highest IC scores are earned by those who can imagine novel solutions to complex problems through the integration of the multiple dimensions of the issue. The parallels between what is valued in ICS and the focus in the deliberative process on considering multiple perspectives, evaluating values, tensions, and trade-offs, and looking for common ground for action, seemed to make ICS an ideal methodology for assessing the value of the Democracy Fellows' exposure to deliberation. Experiences that challenge people's world views or create dissonance between their beliefs and new information they are exposed to can lead them to make more cognitively complex judgments as a way of resolving the tension. Education and other significant life events can also have an impact on the complexity of one's thinking about issues (Neuman 1981; Suedfeld and Bluck 1993). This research suggests that college students exposed to extensive opportunities to deliberate might have higher integrative complexity scores than those who do not.

To test this hypothesis, we scored two questions from the interview for ICS analysis: "What does citizenship mean to you?" and "What do you think are the responsibilities of citizenship?" The coders were blind to whether the response they were coding was from a DF or a CC. We averaged each participant's scores for the two questions and then compared the average IC scores of the DFs with the CCs. As hypothesized, DFs demonstrated significantly higher integrative complexity than did CCs (Table 1). The impact of deliberative training on their long-term ability to think critically and recognize complexity seems clear. All of the participants had the same liberal arts education and had been matched by major, in order to remove those potentially confounding factors. Yet when it came to talking about citizenship and their responsibilities, Democracy Fellows differed to a significant extent from their class cohort.

Table 1: Integrative Complexity Scores in Thinking about Citizenship between Democracy Fellows and the Class Cohort

(M= Mean; SD=Standard Deviation)

Democracy Fellows M (SD)	Class Cohort M (SD)	t	df
3.43 (.71)	2.90 (.79)	2.21*	38

* p < .05

We also wanted to examine potential differences within college majors. Majors were categorized as *political science* or *other*, and differences between the DFs and CCs were examined within these two categories. Again, we averaged each participant's scores for the two questions on citizenship and then compared the average IC scores of the two categories (*political science* and *other*), within the DFs and CCs. As seen in Table 2, differences between DFs and CCs held only with those who did not major in political science. Among alumni who did not major in political science, those who were in the Democracy Fellows program demonstrated significantly more complex thought about the definitions and responsibilities of citizenship than those who did not participate in the DF program.

Table 2: Integrative Complexity in Thinking about Citizenship between Political Science and Nonpolitical Majors in the Democracy Fellows and the Class Cohort

(M=mean; SD=standard deviation)

	Democracy Fellows M (SD)	Class Cohort M (SD)	t	df
Nonpolitical Science Majors	3.54 (.72)	2.69 (.88)	2.68*	24
Political Science Majors	3.21 (.70)	3.29 (.39)	-.236	12

* p < .05.

There was no significant difference between the IC scores of political science majors in either of the study groups. Table 2 tells us that all of the statistically significant difference that we see in the DF/CC comparison in Table 1 is explained by the differences in IC scores of the DFs who did not major in political science. This is important because we would expect students who majored in political science to have spent several years thinking about issues of citizenship and its responsibilities, and to be able to discuss these topics in relatively complex ways, regardless of whether they had learned to deliberate. What this data tells us is that being exposed to deliberative democratic theory, and then learning to deliberate about public policy issues, can teach *nonpolitical science majors* to have similarly complex thinking about citizenship and its responsibilities.

An explanation of how the question, "What does citizenship mean to you?" was scored helps illuminate the differences in scores. IC scores can range from 1 to 7. (We had no 6 or 7 scores for either question, which is not unusual in assessing spoken, rather than written, responses.) In what follows, we provide examples of responses that received each of the different scores, ranging from 1 to 5, with an accompanying explanation of why the response received the particular score that it did.

Scores of 1 indicate that the person sees the answer as one-dimensional and simple. For example, one of our respondents answered by saying, "I guess the first thing that comes to mind is being a citizen of the United States, being a citizen of a certain country." There is no differentiation in this answer. Scores of 2 are given to responses that have some emerging differentiation, but that have no clear second dimension. They hint at the possibility of more, but default to their first point without fully developing a second point. The following statement received a score of 2: "It means that you're an engaged part of society, whether that's at the local or bigger level. But I think it varies from person to person what that engagement means." When respondents demonstrate clear differentiation in their answer, but have not integrated or explained the connection or interaction between those points, they earn a score of 3. An example of an answer scored with a 3 is provided in this response: "I think . . . being a citizen not only means . . . having an identity in a country or nationality or country you associate yourself with, but also being actively engaged in the political process and taking advantage of the rights that are given to you through the social compact." In this 3 score, we see the beginning of what can be identified as components of deliberative thinking. In deliberation, participants are encouraged to recognize that there is more than one way of thinking about something—more than one approach to solving a problem, more than one point of view that has merit in a policy dispute. We expected that Democracy Fellows would be more likely to differentiate than their class cohort, and indeed that is what we found.

In scores of 4 and 5, we find more of the characteristics of deliberation. Scores of 4 are given to answers that have both differentiation and emerging integration. Such an answer might include a statement that ties two differentiated concepts together, or reflects recognition of tensions or trade-offs between the two identified concepts. We scored the following statement as a 4 because it contained both differentiation and emerging integration:

> I think to be a citizen you need to be an active participant in the process of choosing the leaders that are going to represent you— whether that's voting or whether that's getting involved in various political action committees or just making your voice heard in some way. Because, if you don't [do that] you don't really have any chance or any reason . . . to complain legitimately when things don't go your way. So for me, the biggest part is just being an active participant in the governing process.

Scores of 5 (the highest score we gave) are given to responses that include both differentiation and integration, and in which the different pieces are put together to draw some causal conclusion.

> First [it] implies a connection to a particular national identity. I'm a dual citizen of two countries, but I could say that I'm much more of a citizen of one particular country—my additional citizenship is New Zealand because my dad is a New Zealander. But I've only traveled there a couple of times and I was born in the United States and raised here and live here even though I've spent a couple of years abroad. And so, while I'm technically a citizen of both countries, I think citizenship implies a lot more than just the legal connotation. I'm certainly more of a citizen of the United States and I vote here. I reside here, of course. And I follow [US] politics and contribute to my particular community . . . which happens to be the nation's capital—DC. So I think that's my personal understanding of citizenship.

The mean scores of the DFs and the CCs differed because DFs were more likely to get scores that were 3 and above while the more likely range for the CCs was between 1 and 3. Again, it is important to note that these are equally educated young people. The difference is that the DFs, regardless of major, had four years of exposure to discussions of citizenship and deliberation and that experience appears to matter in the way they talk about and understand citizenship and its responsibilities 10 years later. These outcomes reinforce the findings discussed earlier from the interview analysis—that DFs have more complex and multifaceted notions of citizenship.

CITIZENSHIP PRACTICED

A second set of questions inquired into respondents' perceptions of their power to effect change in their social and political environments (see Appendix B). The 2007 study found that Democracy Fellows were more likely to be engaged in political activities on campus and in the community than were members of their class cohort after their first year in school. In order to assess whether this difference still existed, we coded the questions about degree of political engagement using three constructs based on the political science literature about citizen engagement. Relying first on Robert Dahl's categories of citizen engagement, we considered whether the responses could be coded as belonging to either *homo politicus* or *homo civicus* (Dahl 1961). After reading the first set of responses, it seemed clear we needed a third category, which we called *homo cognitio*. There were no participants in the study who said that they did not usually vote, so we saw no need for an additional category of *disengaged/alienated*, which can be found in some nationwide survey analyses.

Homo politicus has an active interest in, and engagement with, politics beyond voting. Respondents in this category see politics as the way to accomplish change and engage in activities such as campaigning, lobbying, actively seeking to influence policy, protesting, and/or donating money to candidates, parties, and/or causes. One of the participants coded as *homo politicus* had this to say about his political engagement:

> Not a lot actually stands in my way [for] political action. . . . I might feel more inclined to give more financially if I had more, but I give about as much as I can. Otherwise I don't know of any major obstacles. I feel empowered to speak when necessary or act when I feel it's necessary. . . . Since graduating I've worked for two members of Congress so the bulk of my professional experience has been in politics.

Homo cognitio thinks it's important to stay informed, and consequently pays attention to the political world, but is not engaged in political activity beyond voting. There were a few people we placed in this category who stayed informed or participated occasionally in political activity when it directly affected their jobs — for example, a health professional who followed health-care policy and might be mobilized to act on that interest, although on no other. Perhaps the best example we had of this view was the interviewee who saw a "difference between being actively involved versus actively knowledgeable. It seems easier to be actively knowledgeable because . . . I can listen to the radio to and from work."

Homo civicus votes, but is otherwise uninterested in politics and/or more preoccupied with work, family, or social activities. The following statement from one of the CCs best exemplifies this perspective:

> I vote and that's it. . . . I [have] the sense that no matter what I
> do it really doesn't matter. . . . At the end of the day, politics is
> controlled by money, so there's really no need to waste my time in
> it. . . . My time is better spent earning money and providing for
> myself than trying to change something that's probably not going
> to change because I don't have enough money to change it.

Categorizing the interviewees in this way produced noticeable differences between the DFs and CCs, as illustrated in Figure 3. Almost half of the DFs were identified as belonging to the *homo politicus* category. Their second most likely category was *homo cognitio*, while the least likely category for them to fall into was *homo civicus*. The most likely category for CCs was *homo cognitio*; the least likely

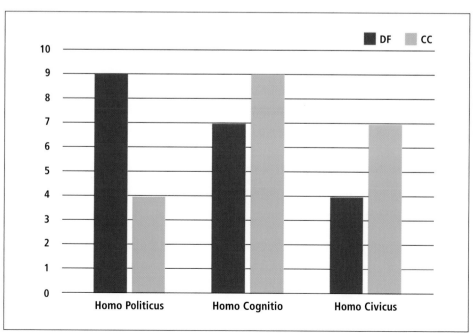

Figure 3: Comparison of DFs and CCs for Measures of Political Activism

category for this group was *homo politicus*. Clearly, DFs continue to be more politically engaged than their class cohort, even when matched by major (there were equal numbers of political science majors in each group). These findings from the interviews were supported by survey data that found a statistically significant difference between the groups, in that there were more DFs *in* or *interested in* pursuing a career in politics or government, and by the fact that more DFs believe running for office is an honorable thing to do.

In addition to putting each of the participants into one of these categories, we coded their responses as "facilitators" or "barriers" to participation, which included personal interest, time, responsibility (or sense of duty), efficacy, knowledge, political conversations with others, social or community context, professional career, and technology/social media. Here again, we found some important differences between the two study groups. As we might expect, given the definitions of each category, respondents that fell into the *homo politicus* and *homo cognitio* groups were more likely to name facilitators for action, while those in the *homo civicus* group were more likely to name barriers.

Democracy Fellows named more facilitators *and* barriers to participation than did the cohort group, reflecting a pattern that we see in the interview data, in which DFs gave longer and more complex answers. For example, DFs were twice as likely as CCs to identify political conversation with others as a political activity, but whether they saw the opportunity for such conversation as a facilitator or a barrier to being engaged depended on the context: it was a facilitator if they were in an environment in which people were trusted or willing to engage across differences, and a barrier if they were in an environment in which people were close-minded or an employment context discouraged such talk. CCs made less mention of political conversations with others as a political activity that they engaged in, but in more of those instances they identified political conversations with others as a facilitator to participation.

One Democracy Fellow engaged in a classic "deliberative" response when asked about things that might stand in the way of political engagement. He had spent most of the past 10 years in politics, working on Capitol Hill and for a presidential campaign in 2008. His response shows the struggle to reconcile what is good in politics with what is bad:

> I think politics has always been a nasty business but the nastiness
> has kind of changed. Not that it's . . . better now or worse then, but
> on the one hand the elections are more fair now . . . than they were,
> say, 50 years ago, and there are probably [fewer] underhanded things
> going on that people don't know about, but the nastiness is . . . just

kind of out there now. . . . I would say that there's way too much discord. . . . I don't like being around people who are absolutely convinced that they are correct. . . . And [those are] the people who are drawn into politics and I think . . . that's a real problem. I think I'm right, but I don't know I'm right—if that makes any sense. I could certainly be wrong about a lot of things . . . and that's why I listen to other people, but I'd say that most of the folks in politics on both sides are not highly deliberative and [are] very much convinced of their own reasoning.

On the other hand, another DF, reflecting another aspect of his deliberative training, saw political conversations in a more positive light:

I get a lot of benefit, I think, from talking with other people about where they come from. I really like the diversity of opinions. . . . I really like being able to discuss civilly a complex and difficult problem. I think that's motivating. [It] makes me want to engage more. . . . I guess I've been more and more encouraged to facilitate these types of political discussions with clients and see where they're coming from and why that may differ from where I am. If I'm able to see where they're coming from, and maybe they see where I'm coming from, then there is certainly something to be gained from that and that's very motivating as well.

DFs were also almost three times as likely as CCs to identify their social or community contexts as important. And among themselves, DFs were substantially more likely to see their communities as facilitators for political action than as barriers, while CCs divided more evenly on this question, listing community as a facilitator five times and as a barrier four times. For example, one DF compared his connection to the community during college with his connection to the community he lives in now:

I think the main difference for me is having the sort of connection to a local politics that really wasn't the case [when I was a university] student in a community I didn't really feel I lived in. . . . It's very difficult to have that sort of town-and-gown relationship. That's totally different now that I feel completely rooted in a community, so I feel much more able to participate in local politics here. The issues mean more to me. So, yeah, I think definitely my interest and participation has gone up.

In contrast, a CC who had some interest in politics coming out of college lost it as a result of living in a town where she felt excluded and devalued:

> We were there for five years—this very backward town in Tennessee. The people were very narrow minded and very sexist and racist and very mean, and it was just really hard to live there. It made me start to believe that no matter what . . . people were just going to be the way they were going to be. . . . As much as I would try to influence them with my own life and—I don't know—make them think differently. . . . I was the first nonwhite person that they'd ever met, most of . . . them. I think that those situations are just really discouraging for me.

DFs also differed from CCs in how they talked about their professional lives and the connection of those lives to their political activity. They named profession/career more than twice as many times as CCs did in this discussion. Interestingly, they were more likely than CCs to name their professions as barriers to political engagement, mostly when talking about what keeps them from being more engaged than they already are. For example, one DF expressed frustration with the way in which his political activity is limited by his job, saying:

> [He had taught] at schools where it was basically forbidden to be politically engaged. I was at a school where a teacher was fired for putting bumper stickers on her car and stuff like that so I've been discouraged from being actively engaged. I'm also married to . . . a journalist, and she's not allowed to be politically engaged, and so . . . [it's been a] frustration.

In some cases, this barrier to action is because respondents have government jobs covered by the Hatch Act, which limits their ability to publicly support candidates.

Others talked about a lack of time as a factor associated with their jobs. One DF who is in graduate school and works in the environmental policy field saw time as a limit on her ability to be engaged with domestic politics:

> It becomes more challenging because you're in a job from eight to five every day. Even as a PhD student . . . I haven't been nearly as involved because it's really, really intensive in terms of studies and research . . . a lot of my work is really international and it requires a lot of international travel. So I would say I'm more involved in global politics and global policies.

For both groups, lack of time due to their jobs, their family life, or their other activities was always seen as a barrier to more political engagement. This is exemplified by the respondent who said that what kept him from being politically involved was "mainly time in terms of career and family. Those are two of the most [important barriers]," he said. "And then after that, extracurricular . . . being involved in my community and/or athletic activities. And so after I do all those things [there is just not enough] time for specific political engagement."

Both groups said they were more likely to be involved when they had a personal interest in an issue, but CCs were more likely than DFs to provide this qualifier to their engagement. This is in keeping with our findings about the broad engagement categories discussed above. Those who fall into the *homo politicus* category are more likely to be interested in, and engaged in, politics across the board and not simply around particular issues that concern them, while *homo cognitio* individuals tend to save their attention and engagement for issues around which they feel a particular personal interest. A similar difference was reflected in the 2007 study where we found that graduating seniors in both groups were likely to say that they would be involved in some way with politics, but DFs were more likely to see that activity as working with others to address problems facing the community, and CCs were more likely to say that they would be involved when they needed to be to protect their interests.

While only small numbers in each group talked about social media as affecting their political engagement (as one interviewee reminded us, Facebook had only just come onto the scene in their senior year), DFs who mentioned it were more likely to see it in a positive light, as enhancing their engagement, than the CCs who mentioned it. It was seen as providing an alternative venue for political participation and as an additional source of political information—both a way to keep up on issues one cares about and a place to make one's voice heard when denied that opportunity in the workplace. For example, one DF who felt stifled at work because of a rigidly apolitical climate "tried having like an alternate identity in Twitter, or I've tried blogging to try and find an outlet where I could speak my mind more freely."

As we noted earlier, this period of young adulthood is a time when many new roles are being learned, most notably those of employee, spouse, and/or parent. We found that these young adults are struggling to balance their careers, families, and personal interests and that for some, more often CCs than DFs, it means that political engagement, other than voting, is a low priority. DFs, by comparison, have managed to stay more involved in the political arena and, when not actively engaged, they are at least "actively knowledgeable."

Because citizenship inherently means having a voice in politics, and because good deliberative practice functions to facilitate voice, we sought to understand whether and how the young adults from the class of 2005 were faring as communicators of their political and social attitudes. We probed for an answer to this question in two different contexts: efficacy and political knowledge.

Speaking Up

Within the context of efficacy, we asked whether they were inclined to express an opinion on political or social issues, and why or why not. To learn how they were acquiring their political knowledge, in addition to mediated sources, such as newspapers, online chats, and late night talk shows, we asked whether they talked to anyone about politics. We were particularly interested in why they chose these political confidantes, and why they avoided others. We also sought to learn how many of these young adults had participated in structured dialogue, and whether they found the experience worthwhile.

The interviewees identified a number of elements that foster their willingness to speak up on public issues. One of the more heartening findings (only slightly more evident among DFs than among CCs) was that they attributed their willingness to speak up to the sense that they were capable, comfortable, and compelled to express themselves. Several attributed that confidence to their Wake Forest education. One DF remarked, "I probably do have more confidence now because I did have such a great experience at Wake and it's really prepared me . . . to speak more eloquently." Others expressed a more general sense of communicative competence, saying they "were very much inclined (to express an opinion)"; "don't have any sort of trepidation or hesitation"; and "feel I can always engage, but it's a choice that I make whether I want to or not."

The two groups were even more closely aligned on the persons or audiences that would encourage their political expression, and it had to do with trust and relationship. One DF summed up the attitudes expressed by many: "I'm usually pretty [much] inclined to express my views and opinions, especially in my family and among friends." A CC echoed that sentiment: "It's more [about] the audience . . . among [my] friends or family or social group . . . I would express my opinion." Both groups were equally clear, however, that there were social/communal situations, that we will describe below, in which they would be inclined to be, as one DF put it, "tight-lipped."

Mirroring the findings about political engagement described in the previous section, an additional catalyst for political expression was personal interest in a particular topic. As one respondent said, "I do take any opportunity that I can to express what I feel and what I believe about a particular issue." Another described it this way:

> I do speak to certain things—more so now. . . . I think that has a lot to do with the work I'm involved in. I'm in the field of education and a lot of students I work with come from low-income backgrounds. . . . Politically and socially the issues of education and poverty are very important so I'm more inclined to speak on [those issues].

One impassioned DF affirmed the importance, sometimes even the responsibility, of speaking up on those matters that are closest to her heart:

> I don't really hesitate [to speak up]. . . . If anything, I'm trying to bring the Socialists in San Francisco back to reality or I'm trying to bring my right-wing conservative Western Pennsylvania family back to the middle. . . . On the whole I express my views because I think I'm not the only one who holds them and I think more people in the middle should speak out.

Despite their overall confidence in their ability to express political opinions, the interviewees did identify conditions that inhibited their willingness to speak up. Frequently referenced by both groups was a prevailing climate of polarization around political discourse. However, the assessment of that climate and its impact on personal expression varied in some interesting ways. First, roughly a fourth of both groups regarded conflict as a deterrent to speaking up: "I'm very cognizant of the world that doesn't want to engage in a respectful manner and I don't usually want to engage in a war in which nobody's mind is going to be changed," or, "I've seen some—I guess I would say—downsides to taking a side or being too polarized or being too quick to vocalize or express [an] opinion." It is important to note, however, that some CCs saw positive aspects to conflict, either because they just enjoyed the debate or because they hoped that sharing differences of opinion could improve the political climate that many find so alienating. One CC represented both of those rationales:

> Part of it is trying to figure out what someone thinks, and why, because that's interesting to me, especially if it's something completely different from what I think [and comes from a] completely different vantage point, political party, association, affiliation, area of the country, or of the world. . . . Hopefully, I can learn something from what they think as opposed to just telling them "you're wrong and I'm right."

There were no DFs who characterized conflict as a positive influence on their willingness to open up about their political or social attitudes. As other data show, it is not that DFs aren't willing to talk with people that they disagree with — indeed, both the survey data and the interviews showed that they were *more* willing to do that than were the CCs. Rather, this finding reflects the DFs' dislike for conflictual talk and their preference for deliberative talk.

Another finding that clearly separated the DFs and CCs was the CCs' identification of social relationships as a deterrent to speaking up about politics; they mentioned twice as often as DFs that they worried about their political expression creating threats to friendships or breaching social conventions. For example, one CC said, "I'm not going to get in fights with people because it's not worth it. I like people; I would like [to] continue being friends with people," and another explained, "When it comes to family and trying to keep the peace, I'm definitely going to try to work at keeping my mouth shut." Still another respondent stated, "People say you don't talk politics and you don't talk religion. And to some extent I have found that to be true."

Both groups essentially agreed that the workplace could be a contentious environment and one generally not conducive to political discussion, with DFs having a slightly more cautionary attitude toward political talk at work than CCs. One DF said, "Probably less (political expression), I think, because I've entered the workforce and realized [that] opinions on hot political issues can affect your advancement [and] other peoples' perceptions of you. . . . I think I was a little naïve when I was in college or [had] just graduated." Others recounted structural restrictions — sometimes even legal prohibitions — to expression: "In terms of public environment or a professional environment, I'm limited by external factors, and it's not that I'm unwilling to express my opinions, but I just am having to gauge the appropriateness or the actual legality of doing so, so therefore I'm fairly limited in those environments."

Those respondents who found the workplace a positive environment to talk politics usually did so because of the nature of their jobs. One DF lawyer remarked:

> I'm more exposed to poverty than I have ever been . . . so it makes me
> more inclined to speak up and I have a connection with my clients.
> I can empathize with them and it does help me speak a little bit more.

Another DF respondent cited the *expectation* of political expression as a component of the job:

I'm not particularly reticent. In fact, in this job I am encouraged to express opinions on the issues that we work on. For example, I contribute to a blog put out by the New York office of our quarterly magazine . . . and sometimes there [are] op-eds in this job so it's very important actually to express an opinion in those pieces.

Pursuit of Political Knowledge

Besides those elements in the lives of these young adults that might compel or constrain them in expressing their own political views, we also hoped to learn whether and how they are inclined to engage others in conversation about politics. Of particular interest is the pursuit of political knowledge, a familiar staple in civic-engagement literature and a variable that had surfaced prominently in early questions about the definition and responsibilities of citizenship.

Initial reads of the responses to this question (a quarter of the transcripts were read before formal coding began with an eye toward motivation for interaction) unearthed three trends we called *confirmation, curiosity,* and *comfort.*

- *Confirmation* describes a respondent's inclination to seek sources and conversational partners whose political attitudes align with his/her own. One stated, "I kind of learned that it's easier to just talk to people who agree with you." Another interviewee elaborated, "I think in many respects it's a sort of preaching-to-the-choir type of thing. I haven't had a great many conversations with someone whose views are opposed to mine in politics."

- *Curiosity,* on the other hand, describes an interest in, or desire to, understand different perspectives or gain a balanced understanding of an issue. Also coded as curiosity were comments indicating that pure enjoyment of political dialogue motivated discussion. Two different participants describe this motivation for political talk: "I enjoy talking to my friends who have opposite beliefs," and "My parents have kind of found this very intense conservatism so it's really interesting to hear their points of view and debate and discuss."

- *Comfort* reflects a response in which the participant states that he/she chooses to talk politics with people who are regarded as "safe" and allow him/her to be authentic—in short, do not judge him/her for particular beliefs and opinions. When identifying and explaining the choices of people with whom to talk politics, one respondent remarked, "Those are the people I interact with on a day-to-day basis and I would feel comfortable with." Another said, "I think because I trust it's sort of a safe environment—that I'm not going to be judged for my views."

We began this line of inquiry with a general question, mirroring the survey, about the respondent's sources of political information and knowledge. The question yielded a wide array of sources that could not easily be categorized as representing one particular point of view. Most respondents simply listed multiple sources, but about one-quarter of them—and twice as many DFs as CCs—explicitly commented that they deliberately sought information from a range of sources in order to get different viewpoints; a balanced perspective; or neutral, unbiased information.

DFs and CCs named similar numbers of people or groups of people on whom they relied for political information and conversation. For both groups, the most important reasons given for talking to those sources about politics had to do with (1) the potential to gain knowledge in the absence of adequate information on an issue and (2) curiosity—the desire to understand different, even oppositional, perspectives.

The desire to gain knowledge in and of itself was both a facilitator of, and a barrier to, political conversation. Our respondents often talked to people from whom they felt they could learn something, and sometimes avoided talking to people when they were skeptical that credible knowledge would be gleaned from doing so. For example, one CC said, "The common thread [in why I talk to sources] is they're people whose opinions I respect because I know that they are well informed and make efforts to inform themselves." In contrast, a DF preferred not to talk to others about politics or use them as sounding boards because, "I think getting news from other people is like [getting] secondhand news and if somebody does say, 'Oh, did you hear about blah, blah, blah,' I would probably say I'll look it up myself and try to verify that information." In short, respondents sought information in the absence of adequate knowledge on an issue, but they were clear that their conversational efforts should not be wasted on sources whose credibility was suspect.

Curiosity, on the other hand, was virtually always a facilitator of political conversation. For example, one DF explained why he talked to his sources: "I guess I value their opinions and I like to get their viewpoints, especially when it comes to family. A lot of the opinions are very diverse and it's actually kind of fun sometimes to have a nice political conversation. We know that we're not going to agree . . . but we prepare our points and we work things out and I guess we like to debate a little bit."

Interestingly, although both curiosity and the desire to gain knowledge were the top reasons given for motivating political conversation by both DFs and CCs, the order of these reasons was reversed for the two groups. Curiosity was the most common reason given by DFs (13 mentions, compared to 9 mentions by CCs) and desire for knowledge was the topmost reason given by CCs (12 mentions, compared to 8 by DFs). Furthermore, among CCs, polarization was offered as commonly as was a desire for credible knowledge as a reason for talking to, or avoiding talk, with others. As one CC explained:

> Most [of] the people that I talk politics with are folks who I know I can have a conversation [with] without [their] getting upset or offended, [though] I wouldn't say I choose friends based on their political stance. I have some friends who share [my] views and I have some who don't, but most are always willing to have an open dialogue. . . . I really look for folks who have their own opinions but are willing to have an open discussion and not be judgmental or so solidified in their position that they are going to shut down.

Half as many DFs as CCs referred to the potential for polarizing or combative interactions as a reason for the sources chosen or avoided. It seems that DFs are, overall, somewhat more accepting of, even interested in, engaging in dialogue with individuals whose perspectives differ from their own. They are less likely to fear an argument and more likely to enjoy political discussion, especially when they think they will learn something from it.

As Figure 4 demonstrates, more evidence in support of this conclusion comes from respondents' referencing *confirmation* or *comfort* as motivations for choosing or avoiding sources. CCs were about equally likely to mention *confirmation* and *comfort* as they were *curiosity*. As illustrated in the following comment from a CC, sometimes talking to people who could confirm one's own views was at the same time a safe or *comforting* conversational context:

> I guess [I talk to people] not necessarily by choice; kind of by default. They're the people who I'm around the most [when politics] . . . comes up in conversation. I guess history has shown my friends and family that it's a safe environment. . . . We all have the same opinion or views, so we are comfortable having the conversation.

In contrast, DFs were much less likely to mention *confirmation* or *comfort* than they were *curiosity* and, overall, less likely to mention both *confirmation* and *comfort* than were CCs.

Figure 4: Differences in Motivations for Talking about Politics with Others

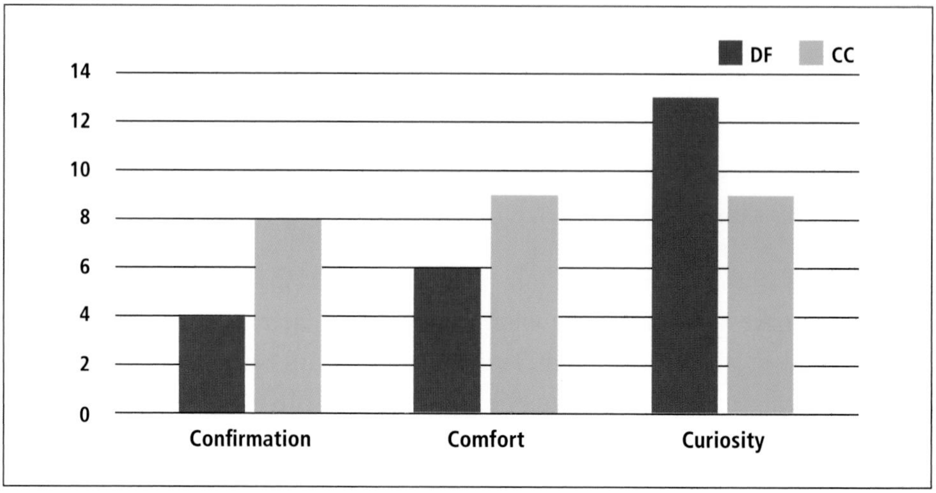

POLITICS REASSESSED

The 2007 study concluded that at graduation, Democracy Fellows had a more sophisticated view of the political system and were actually more critical of how politics was practiced than were their fellow students in the class cohort. We also found that, across the board, students in both groups were turned off by the degree of polarization and the influence of money in politics.

We asked the 2015 interviewees what they would change about how politics is currently practiced if they had the power to do so. Based on the earlier findings, we hypothesized that DFs would be more likely to identify the "hidden" or structural causes of political dysfunction than would CCs, again because of the evidence of more complex thinking on this subject, but we also expected to see relatively equal levels of concern about money and polarization.

Our hypotheses were borne out by the findings. Structural changes to such practices as the Electoral College and gerrymandered voting districts were the most frequently mentioned reforms DFs would like to see. As one DF stated:

> As much as I like what the Founding Fathers did, I think our system
> is broken. I don't like the two-party system. It . . . forces us to take
> one side or the other, and there are lots of people [who] would rath-
> er pick "none of the above." In a parliamentary system you have to
> build coalitions or, when a party gets 17 percent of the vote, [it gets]
> approximately 17 percent of [the] representatives. If you don't have
> that avenue you're essentially silencing a large percentage of the
> population, and I think that's a problem.

The next two changes most frequently sought by DFs were in the role of money and the degree of polarization between the parties and among people (often attributed to the structural deficiencies mentioned above). With regard to the role of money, one DF stated:

> What I would change if I had any power would be to reform how
> campaign finance takes place. I would like to try to reduce the amount
> of money in politics. [Ideally I'd like to see] politics without so many
> connections to donations and corporations that are putting money
> into . . . politics.

And speaking to the degree of polarization of people and politics, another DF said:

> I can't claim to be an expert on how things work, but people could just use a bit more common sense. . . . Obviously no one side is going to get it completely right or be completely wrong but if people could find a middle road and just divorce themselves from [those with] extremist views (the ones [who] speak the loudest)—if we could do a little bit more listening [to views in the middle] . . . and [a little bit more] compromising, that would be awesome.

Figure 5 demonstrates the contrast between DFs and CCs with regard to where they think changes should be made. CCs were more likely to focus on the people in office, most urgently wishing to end the polarization among the parties and to change the officeholders; there was little recognition in this group that the behaviors they disliked were in some way linked to structural problems in the political process. For example, a CC interviewee stated, "I would just want to clean house. I'd want to look at some representatives and some Congress members [who] have been around too long and look at starting with a fresh bunch," while another interviewee proposed, "really trying to get people in the office [who are] about the work and about doing something for the betterment of society . . . and not necessarily just for themselves and their friends."

Figure 5: Comparison of DF and CC Views of Major Problems in America's Political System

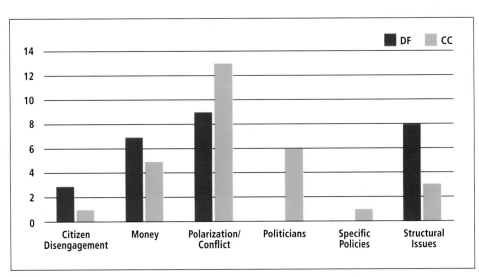

CCs were also concerned about the role of money, as exemplified by this response:

> I would get the money out of politics. I think we need publicly funded elections and I think that would [help make] politics far more reflective of voters' concerns rather than donors' concerns. . . . A lot of money goes to buying media outlets, media consultants, and polling consultants. What ends up happening is [that] politics becomes a commodity.

Only three CCs mentioned structural issues. While encouraging more civic engagement by average people was low on the list of both groups, DFs were more likely to mention it than CCs. As one DF explained:

> I would try to make it [politics] more accessible to regular people. I think it's very daunting for a person to get involved, especially with political parties the way they are. I go to a monthly meeting that's actually very friendly for a political party meeting, but I think people get intimidated by process and I wish it were a little more open and people could see what goes on. I also wish the electoral process was not as punishing.

The adult political socialization literature suggests that the new roles taken on by young adults often have an impact on the way they think about politics and their civic roles. We wondered, in particular, whether the stronger sense of civic/political efficacy that we found in Democracy Fellows, compared to their class cohort, was still present a decade later after they had entered the work world, started families, and settled in communities. We asked them about their perception of their ability to make a difference or affect change in three different environments: their communities, their workplaces, and the political arena. We coded their responses as either positive or negative expressions of personal efficacy. That determined whether they could have an impact. We also looked for possible explanations of these views.

We found virtually no difference between the two groups in their responses to these questions. Both groups were most likely to feel efficacious in their communities and least likely to feel efficacious in the national political arena. This example of positive efficacy in the community setting was offered by one of the respondents:

> I feel in my social and community life that I have a really good ability to [effect change]. You choose some of that to a certain degree

depending on where you're living and depending on where you decide to rent or buy. . . . You're really choosing the community to a certain degree. Because I can be involved and go to meetings for my community and it tends to be a place where I can speak out, I feel I could make change or I can at least make my voice heard.

In contrast, when asked about their ability to have an impact in the political arena, there was much more negativity. One CC said, "As one person who is not involved and [doesn't] necessarily have a reputation or really the experience to speak about certain things, I would say [my ability to effect change] is probably pretty low."

Efficacy in the workplace tended to depend on the kind of job they had (those with political jobs felt more politically efficacious), the size of the organization they worked for, and their place in the organizational hierarchy. Positive efficacy related to the size of the organization as exemplified by this statement:

I've kind of earned a position of respect where I work and my opinion is very much valued. . . . I work in a very small organization and there's not a lot of bureaucracy where I work so there are a few key decision makers and I think if I were to bring a well-reasoned idea to the team it would be well received and I would have a lot of power in affecting that.

Jobs in the political realm also contribute to positive statements of efficacy:

I think I'm a little bit biased since I work in politics. I have a better idea of . . . how politics works and how some of these bureaucracies work. So I feel I have a decent handle on how I'd want to accomplish something. . . . But I don't think most people have that insight and so I think more than most . . . I have a better idea of how to effect change or how to increase the odds of effecting change.

Both groups had comparable levels of positive efficacy, most frequently stated when they talked about their ability to have an impact in their communities and, to a lesser extent, their jobs. This positive sense of personal efficacy was most frequently associated with statements about speaking up on issues and about their ability to have an impact by joining groups in which their voices would be multiplied and magnified. For example:

I think I have the ability to choose what group I devote my time to, and . . . how much time I give and to what causes. . . . I don't know how much . . . influence I have as an individual but I think when a group of like-minded motivated people get together that's when your voice is a little bit louder.

I think I've been around long enough in politics that I know some politicians personally. . . . I also now have a large network of friends. Both [groups] I think would listen to what I believe in. I think we can mobilize and do things if we really needed to effect a little bit of change and we would at least be heard.

The two groups also felt comparable levels of lower efficacy when they talked about the political arena, in which they identified structural issues most frequently as the cause of their negative feelings. In particular, they tended to differentiate between local and national politics, feeling more able to effect change locally and least able to do so nationally. One DF distinguished between levels of government and efficacy this way:

I've worked in the District of Columbia and in Maryland and I think that I had some influence over some of the policies around child welfare in the District of Columbia, based on my work there. We're working on some basically educational advocacy in the school that my clients attend now and I feel we've had a lot of ability to change the . . . political climate of that particular school. I don't have connections to any state senators or national senators. . . . You can let your congressman or senator know your view but I think there's a lot more politics of . . . who-you-know involved at the higher levels. And so in that way I feel very disconnected.

Another respondent talked about the lack of responsiveness of public officials to people like them. A CC stated:

So much of what goes on right now in politics really just has to do with people pushing their own individual agendas and not really doing what is being brought to their attention by citizens. I think it's a lot of legislators [who] are influenced by lobbyists and I see that in my little sector of education. I definitely have my doubts about [my ability to have] an impact on the political [scene] . . . those people are going to be influenced by who they want to be influenced by and it's definitely not me.

The one difference between the two groups was that Democracy Fellows were more likely than their class cohort to associate knowledge with feelings of efficacy. A DF said, "I feel I've been educated [in] the issues and I'm informed so in that way I feel knowledge is power." For the DFs, *lack* of knowledge could also function to limit one's influence. A DF who works in the environmental policy area felt that she could effect change in that area, but:

> When it comes to expressing my opinion and trying to influence the health-care debate, I feel [as though] I have no power in that. And I don't think anybody would care either what I had to say. But then on other things where my expertise and my experience [are] valued, I feel I have more of an influence.

We also asked the respondents about whether they felt they had more or less power than they had when they first graduated from college. Here again, there were no noticeable differences between the two groups, but their responses reflected the way in which their real-world experiences had impacted their sense of having power.

One DF noted a stronger sense of efficacy since leaving college that he attributed to both being part of a community and to his profession as a teacher:

> Because I'm a teacher I have [the] ability to speak to others, where as a student you didn't have that ability. People didn't automatically listen to you. For a living, people listen to me every day. . . . I don't blab on about politics all the time, but you have that ability to trickle down those sorts of ideas in your classroom. . . . At the same time I think because I'm part of this community, and I own a home here, I feel I have . . . agency to make change. People take you more seriously when you're a part of a community. You're not a student living in a dorm who doesn't really interact with issues outside of the university campus. . . . I definitely feel [those are] the main changes: being out there and then, of course, having access to people who are listening to what you have to say.

Echoing a theme found in many of the responses, another DF talked about having developed a more realistic view of what was possible in politics:

> I think . . . when I graduated I was idealistic and things seemed like they should be a lot more simple than they actually turn out to be; there's a lot more politics involved in politics—if that makes any sense —than what you're really aware of. It's harder to influence change than you would expect or, really, than it should be.

A CC drew this contrast between the book learning gained in college and learning that comes from actual experience:

> I think I have been out in the real world more. . . . I think that when we learn about it in school we . . . read these books [that tell us] this is the process, and if you go through this process this is how a bill becomes a law and all you have to do is propose this bill and then one day it'll be a law. No, that's not how it works and even things that we all know are good, don't end up the way we think they should. . . . I've probably just become—I don't know if "less trusting" is the right [term]—but just more discerning perhaps.

While the interviews revealed similar levels of personal efficacy, it is important to note that on one standard measure of efficacy assessed in the survey data, the CCs differed from the DFs. In response to the statement, "People like me don't have a say about what the government does," CCs were more likely than DFs to agree to a statistically significant degree.

EDUCATING FOR CITIZENSHIP

The power of the Democracy Fellows' experience came out clearly again in a set of questions we asked all of the respondents about how well they thought their university had prepared them for serving their community and being politically active. We also asked them to identify their most helpful civic experiences. Both groups tended to give the university some credit for preparing them to serve their community and to be politically active, focusing far more on positive experiences than on negative ones. However, they differed along several lines when it came to identifying the factors they thought were important in their civic education.

The class cohort identified the campus culture twice as often as Democracy Fellows as a facilitator of their civic learning. CCs were particularly focused on this in response to the question about their preparation to serve the community. They talked about the university as a place where they had been strongly encouraged to buy into the Wake Forest mission related to doing good and helping others, and about the numerous organizational opportunities they had, especially through Greek organizations, to carry out such service. They also mentioned organizational life as being important more frequently than DFs and were far more likely than DFs to identify their service experiences as the most helpful civic preparation. In fact, service activities for CCs were the most frequently named activities elicited in answer to the questions about how their education had prepared them for civic life.

In contrast, the Democracy Fellows were much less likely to name campus culture as a facilitator of their engagement, and when they did talk about it, they were almost as likely to see it as a negative as they were to see it as a positive. Positive references to the campus culture by both groups tended to focus on a culture that encouraged civic engagement, especially service, and on the wealth of opportunities for such involvement. Negative references to the campus culture by both groups tended to focus on what was termed the Wake Forest "bubble," both as it described the university's separation from the city and the "real world," and as it defined a sense of entitlement/privilege or political apathy. These statements by DFs capture this concern:

> The thing I think about it is that my college education was a private
> school . . . there's a certain amount of entitlement . . . or pampering

that came from that environment that I think sometimes I didn't realize I had developed.

We used to call it the Wake bubble because students tend to kind of stay within their bubble on campus to the point [where] sometimes you forget there are elderly people in the world. You forget there are two-year-olds. All you see are basically 17-22 year olds . . . and for the most part [they all] seem to have affluent backgrounds . . . and I think we kind of forget how to interact, communicate, and work with people of different backgrounds, whether . . . racial, or social, or economic or age-related.

The Democracy Fellows were most likely to name the DF experience as the most helpful preparation for civic life (15 of the 20) and every DF mentioned it in response to at least one of the questions. In one of the explanations of its value, one DF talked about the importance of the fact that the program extended over the full four years, starting with the First-Year Seminar:

I just think it's so valuable . . . to teach students at 18 [when they're] independent for the first time, to give them the skills of how to have a conversation and how to listen to what people are saying and how to take feedback and . . . to understand the diversity of viewpoints [without hating those] other persons for what they said and recognizing what a difference of opinion really means. I think that's the crux of deliberative democracy. And if everybody had that kind of training and education, imagine how much more productive society would be. . . . If I [hadn't been in] that program, no way would I have learned any of that in college and it's just unfortunate that there were only—what—30 of us?

Beyond the DF program, the next most commonly mentioned element of their college experience DFs deemed helpful in furthering their civic engagement was the academic preparation they received at Wake Forest. In sharp contrast to the CCs, who listed service as their "most helpful" experiences, service came in a distant fourth for the DFs. This finding replicates the 2007 research that found the CCs to be more engaged in community service and the DFs more engaged in political activity.

While both groups gave academics (their major; particular teachers or courses; or more generally, learning how to think critically) a lot of credit for preparing them, the Democracy Fellows were substantially more likely to mention it overall and in a positive light than were CCs. Negative views made up the majority of CC responses. Criticisms of academics tended to focus on the lack of opportunity for practical application and real-world experience. For example, one CC noted, "There's the academic version of things and then there's real world in a lot of cases," when asked about whether he had been prepared to be politically active. Another student said:

> I just think that [in] a lot of the courses and a lot of the classwork . . . we were talking about theories at a high level but being able to take that from that point to really act on it . . . there wasn't really that connection. So it was more studying and understanding . . . of the [historical perspectives] and issues and concerns . . . but to really take that and hit the ground running and go to work and do something with it as far as in the community, that was a disconnect.

Others, who had not majored in political science, tended to identify the sheer lack of discussion about politics and civic life in any of their classes, particularly if they had majored in the natural sciences.

Very few of the study participants mentioned service-learning experiences that occur in the classroom and strategically tie service assignments to theory and practice, but where it was mentioned, it was seen in a very positive light, particularly as a way to overcome the isolation of students from the community. One of the CCs talked about it this way:

> Those kids that we worked with—a disadvantaged, low socioeconomic group of kids—I'd say if I hadn't had that experience then I would not have been prepared to do what I do now, which is working with diverse student populations. I think in my case I was lucky because I had that experience, but I could see where if I had not worked with the disadvantaged population at some point, and being a Wake Forest grad and part of the Wake Forest bubble, I think [it] would have been even more jarring when I went on to work.

In summary, interview data reflected, and survey data confirmed, that more DFs than CCs felt prepared for an active civic life, whether in their communities or in the political arena.

ANALYSIS OF THE SURVEY DATA

We constructed a survey that participants could take online (see Appendix C). Following their interviews, participants were sent an e-mail with a link to the survey. All participants completed the survey. The survey was constructed primarily from existing scales (Bobek et al. 2009; Flanagan et al. 2007; Lopez et al. 2006) measuring the following constructs:

- Involvement in traditional venues of political action vs. service activities

- Active vs. passive citizenship

- Views of the political process and one's role in it

- Sense of political efficacy, and voice

- Communal vs. individualistic political language, outlook, and motivation

- Views of, and attitudes toward, deliberation and applying deliberative knowledge

- Political ideology

- Impact of higher education on citizenship

- Demographics

As with the ICS analysis, we compared the responses of DFs and CCs. A summary of the significant differences appears in Table 3.

Survey results indicated that, compared to CCs, the DFs were more politically engaged; more comfortable communicating about politics (even with those whose opinions differed from their own); higher in some aspects of political efficacy; more likely to believe running for office was an honorable thing to do; and more likely to be in, or interested in, a career that involved politics or government. DFs were also more likely than CCs to say that their college education prepared them to serve their community and to be active politically.

Table 3: Significant Differences between Democracy Fellows (DF) and the Class Cohort (CC)

Survey Item	Result
Read a newspaper for information on politics and current events	DF>CC
People like me don't have a say about what the government does	CC>DF
Running for office is an honorable thing to do	DF > CC
I am in, or interested in, pursuing a career in politics and government	DF > CC
Communicate with Others about Politics • I talk to other people about politics • I'm interested in other people's opinion about politics, even if those opinions are different from my views • I encourage others to express their opinions about politics, even if those opinions are different from my views • I am interested in talking about politics and political issues	DF > CC
Degree to which your college education prepared you to serve your community	DF > CC
Degree to which your college education prepared you to be active politically	DF > CC

Other findings of note for the entire sample provide context for these differences, as well as some confirmation of the role of a college education more generally. All of our participants were registered to vote, and only 1 out of 40 of our study participants reported not voting in the most recent presidential election. The mean for "current likelihood to vote on a regular basis" was 4.87 out of 5. In addition, 68 percent of the sample considered themselves to be "politically engaged or politically active."

Reflecting national trends that show millennials to be more likely to favor Democrats over Republicans, the respondents, overall, described themselves as more liberal (59 percent) than conservative (23 percent), with 18 percent describing themselves as moderate in their political views. Overall, about two-thirds (72.5 percent) affiliated more with the Democratic than the Republican Party (ranging from "Independent, leans Democrat" to "Strong Democrat") and about one-fourth affiliated more with the Republican Party; 5 percent claimed "Independent, does not lean either way." Although there were no statistically significant differences in political leaning between DFs and CCs, if anything DFs leaned in a more conservative direction than did the CCs (30 percent of the DFs described themselves as conservative; 30 percent affiliated more strongly with the Republican Party). Thus, the impact of the DF experience was not to influence individuals in a more liberal direction.

Again reflecting national trends, there was very high involvement among CCs and DFs alike in doing volunteer work in their communities (M=4.05 on a 5-point scale), and high endorsement of the importance of helping the less fortunate (M=4.63), of helping others in one's community (M=4.53), and of believing community service work to be honorable (M=4.78). Participants in both groups also placed high importance on challenging inequities in society (M=4.03).

DFs and CCs alike obtained news about politics and current events from the Internet (M=3.70 on a 4-point scale), although as noted above, DFs were more likely to read a newspaper.

Overall, participants in both groups felt efficacious regarding civic action (M=4.36 on a 5-point scale). For example, if these college-educated young adults "found out about a problem in their community that they wanted to do something about," they felt highly capable of the following actions: organizing and running a meeting (M=4.45), expressing views in front of a group (M=4.7), identifying individuals who could help solve the problem (M=4.43), writing an opinion letter to a local newspaper (M=4.58), phoning someone one had never met to get help (M=4.35), and contacting an elected official about the problem (M=4.55). They felt very comfortable signing e-mail or written petitions that supported views they held (M=4.37) and expressing their views in front of a group (M=4.15). Most participants (80 percent) had signed an online petition at some point.

Most participants (85 percent) had advocated for a particular candidate in conversations with others during an election. A majority had donated money to a political campaign or cause (75 percent), written an e-mail or letter advocating for a political position or opinion (65 percent), or had attended a political rally or demonstration (62.5 percent). Extremely few (20 percent), however, had worked as canvassers for a political or social group or a candidate. Almost all disagreed with the statement "It really doesn't matter to me who the president is" (M=1.53 on a 5-point scale). They mostly agreed that politics has become too partisan (M=4.58).

Overall, there was extremely low endorsement of ideas reflecting unconditional support of government or its policies. For example, there was very strong disagreement with the following statements: "Newspapers should not criticize the government" (M=1.38), "I support all US policies no matter what" (M=1.42), and "It is un-American to criticize the government" (M=1.43).

The survey results reinforce the qualitative data gained from the interviews. They also reflect national trends for this age group. Consequently, the survey contributes to our confidence that the differences we find between the two groups are meaningful and have something to say about the power of deliberative training.

IMPLICATIONS FOR
HIGHER EDUCATION

I n this report, we began with a summary of our findings and then explained in more detail how we arrived at those findings through a further elaboration of our interview and survey data. As we close, we want to reflect on the implications of these findings for higher education institutions.

It is no small feat to demonstrate the 10-year-long impact of a specific type of experience on outcomes as complex as complexity of thinking, interest and comfort in engaging in dialogue with others over differences, curiosity about the opinions and experiences of others, and views of politics. Consider the many factors working against the likelihood of identifying a noticeable long-term impact of this particular program. These were college students, whose development in these areas had already been shaped to some extent by earlier childhood experiences in their families, peer groups, and schools. Furthermore, a four-year college education in itself influences these same characteristics. The DF program, while sustained and significant, was only a small portion of the students' college experiences, so it is perfectly plausible to assume that it would not have had a particularly notable impact over 10 years. Additionally, in the decade after leaving school, graduates are bombarded by many competing influences, embodied in the significant transitions related to their careers, geographic location, peer groups, and family status. Finally, we recognized from the beginning that we were working with a small sample size, which limits the power to detect statistically significant differences. And yet, despite all these factors, we did discover noticeable—and even statistically significant—differences between groups.

The fact that meaningful differences between the DFs and CCs persist a decade after their college graduation provides further evidence that exposure to, and training in, deliberative dialogue is a high-impact practice for developing engaged citizens who are adept at working across differences. Admittedly, there is more research to be done to gain insight into the aspects of the program that are most important to achieving these results. How many deliberations are enough to make an impact? What is the impact and importance of curricular vs. extracurricular components? Is it important to begin these experiences in the first year of college? Might the impact be lessened—or increased—by waiting until students have some college experience under their belts? With all the nuances of the process that were taught, what were the ones that got the most traction, made the most impact, created the staying power over 10-15 years? We could go on. These findings have whetted our appetite for more knowledge.

Still, the significance of the current findings suggests we should not wait for more data to begin to act on the data we have. Even at this point, it would seem that for institutions of higher education that value these outcomes, there is a strong case to be made that deliberation should be institutionalized in curricular and cocurricular experiences. And it seems that most institutions of higher education would value outcomes affected by the Democracy Fellows' experiences. Outcomes such as making a positive difference in society and for humanity, critical thinking, communication, inquiry and analysis, creative thinking, intercultural learning, and social relevance are common in educational mission statements and desired competencies. Many higher education institutions today are struggling with problems related to understanding and communicating across differences. Our state and federal governments are making little progress in solving important social problems because of polarization and gridlock. The ability to solve problems with others who have different experiences and viewpoints about those problems requires comfort with complexity, as well as the motivation and ability to talk productively about those issues. Our data suggest that these outcomes are promoted when college students learn the theory and practice of deliberative dialogue. We can imagine many ways that such experiences can be institutionalized: first- or second-year seminars; annual community dialogues organized and moderated by students; training of faculty to promote incorporation of dialogue across the curriculum; training of student leaders, such as resident assistants and peer advisors; and use of deliberation more widely in institutional decision making. Institutionalization need not be structured exactly like the DF program was, although we suspect that sustained exposure, rather than one-shot opportunities, and a curricular component that gives students a framework for understanding and analyzing what they are learning, combined with practice outside of the classroom, are keys to replicating these outcomes. Higher education is the perfect place for this kind of experience and education because not only do we value the outcomes, but we also have the luxury of time to provide sustained experience at an important developmental stage in the lives of our students. Our 15-year experiment has ended. But the results suggest that continued experimentation and institutionalization of deliberative dialogue training is a worthwhile endeavor if one believes, as we do, that part of the mission of higher education is to prepare students for their civic lives.

REFERENCES

ASHE (Association for the Study of Higher Education). "Research on Outcomes and Processes of Inter-group Dialogue." *Higher Education Report* 34 (4) (2006): 59–73.

Bauerlein, Mark. *The Dumbest Generation: How the Digital Age Stupefies Young Americans and Jeopardizes Our Future.* New York: Penguin, 2008.

Bobek, Deborah, Jonathan Zaff, Yibing Li, and Richard M. Lerner. "Cognitive, Emotional, and Behavioral Components of Civic Action: Towards an Integrated Measure of Civic Engagement." *Journal of Applied Developmental Psychology* 30 (5) (2006): 615–627.

Buss, Terry F., and C. Richard Hofstetter. "Communication, Information and Participation During an Emerging Crisis." *Social Science Journal* 18 (1981): 81–91.

CIRCLE, NCoC, HIoP, and Mobilize.org. *Millennials Civic Health Index.* Washington, DC: National Conference on Citizenship, et al., 2013. http://www.ncoc.net/MillennialsCHI (accessed August 26, 2016).

Dahl, Robert. *Who Governs? Democracy and Power in an American City.* New Haven, CT: Yale University Press, 1961.

Dedrick, John R., Laura Grattan, and Harris Dienstfrey, eds. *Deliberation and the Work of Higher Education: Innovations for the Classroom, the Campus, and the Community.* Dayton, OH: Kettering Foundation Press, 2008.

Delli Carpini, Michael X., Fay Lomax Cook, and Lawrence R. Jacobs. "Public Deliberation, Discursive Participation, and Citizen Engagement." *Annual Review of Political Science* 7 (2004): 315–344.

Delli Carpini, Michael X., and Scott Keeter. *What Americans Know about Politics and Why It Matters.* New Haven, CT: Yale University Press, 1996.

Easton, David, and Jack Dennis. *Children in the Political System.* New York: McGraw-Hill, 1969.

Flanagan, Constance, and Peter Levine. "Civic Engagement and the Transition to Adulthood." *The Future of Children* 20 (1) (2010): 159–179.

Flanagan, Constance, Amy K. Syvertsen, and Michael D. Stout. *Civic Measurement Models: Tapping Adolescents' Civic Engagement.* CIRCLE Working Paper #55, 2007. www.civicyouth.org/PopUps/WorkingPapers/WP55Flannagan.pdf (accessed August 26, 2016).

Gastil, John. *Political Communication and Deliberation.* Los Angeles: Sage Publishing, 2008.

Greenberg, Eric H., and Karl Weber. *Generation We: How Millennial Youth Are Taking Over America and Changing Our World Forever.* Emeryville, CA: Pachatusan, 2008.

Greenstein, Fred. *Children and Politics.* New Haven, CT: Yale University Press, 1965.

Gurin, Patricia, Biren A. Nagda, and Nicholas Sorensen. "Intergroup Dialogue: Education for a Broad Conception of Civic Engagement." *Liberal Education* 97 (2) (2011): 46–51.

Harriger, Katy J., and Jill J. McMillan. *Speaking of Politics: Preparing College Students for Democratic Citizenship through Deliberative Dialogue.* Dayton, OH: Kettering Foundation Press, 2007.

Hess, Diana E. *Controversy in the Classroom: The Democratic Power of Discussion.* New York: Routledge, 2009.

Ho, Daniel E., Kosuke Imai, Gary King, and Elizabeth A. Stuart. "Matching as Nonparametric Preprocessing for Reducing Model Dependence in Parametric Causal Inference." *Political Analysis* 15, (2007): 199–236.

Hollander, Elizabeth, and Cathy Burack. *How Young People Develop Long-Lasting Habits of Civic Engagement: A Conversation on Building a Research Agenda.* The Spencer Foundation, 2009. http://www.compact.org/wp-content/uploads/2009/05/spencerconversationresearchagenda1.pdf (accessed August 26, 2016).

Jennings, M. Kent, and Richard G. Niemi. *The Political Character of Adolescence: The Influence of Families and Schools.* Princeton, NJ: Princeton University Press, 1974.

Kiesa, Abby, Alexander P. Orlowski, Peter Levine, Deborah Both, Emily H. Kirby, Mark H. Lopez, and Karlo B. Marcelo. *Millennials Talk Politics: A Study of College Student Political Engagement.* College Park, MD: CIRCLE, 2007.

Levine, Peter. "What Do We Know about Civic Engagement?" *Liberal Education* 97 (2) (2011): 1.

London, Scott. *Doing Democracy: How a Network of Grass Roots Organizations Is Strengthening Community, Building Capacity, and Shaping a New Kind of Civic Education.* Dayton, OH: Kettering Foundation Press, 2010.

Lopez, Mark H., Peter Levine, Deborah Both, Abby Kiesa, Emily Kirby, and Karlo Marcelo. *The 2006 Civic and Political Health of the Nation: A Detailed Look at How Youth Participate in Politics and Communities*. CIRCLE, 2006. www.civicyouth.org/ PopUps/2006_CPHS_Report_update.pdf (accessed August 26, 2016).

Mathews, David, and Noëlle McAfee. *Making Choices Together: The Power of Public Deliberation*. Dayton, OH: Kettering Foundation, 2003.

Mutz, Diana C. "Is Deliberative Democracy a Falsifiable Theory?" *Annual Review of Political Science* 11 (2008): 521–538.

Nabatchi, Tina. "Addressing the Citizenship and Democratic Deficits: Exploring the Potential of Deliberative Democracy for Public Administration." *American Review of Public Administration* 40 (4) (2010a): 376–399.

Nabatchi, Tina. "Deliberative Democracy and Citizenship: In Search of the Efficacy Effect." *Journal of Public Deliberation* 6 (2) (2010b): 1–47.

Nabatchi, Tina, John Gastil, Matt Leighninger, and G. Michael Weiksner, eds. *Democracy in Motion: Evaluating the Practice and Impact of Deliberative Civic Engagement*. New York: Oxford University Press (2012).

National Task Force on Civic Learning and Democratic Engagement. *A Crucible Moment: College Learning and Democracy's Future*. AAC&U, 2012. https://www. aacu.org/sites/default/files/files/crucible/Crucible_508F.pdf (accessed August 26, 2016).

Neuman, W. Russell "Differentiation and Integration: Two Dimensions of Political Thinking." *American Journal of Sociology* 86 (1981): 1236–1268.

Niemeyer, Simon. "The Emancipatory Effect of Deliberation: Empirical Lessons from Mini-Publics." *Politics and Society* 39 (1) (2011): 103–140.

Schlozman, Kay L., Sidney Verba, and Henry E. Brady. *The Unheavenly Chorus: Unequal Political Voice and the Broken Promise of American Democracy*. Princeton, NJ: Princeton University Press, 2012.

Sigel, Roberta S., ed. *Political Learning in Adulthood: A Sourcebook of Theory and Research*. Chicago: University of Chicago Press, 1989.

Sigel, Roberta S., and Marilyn B. Hoskin. *The Political Involvement of Adolescents*. New Brunswick, NJ: Rutgers University Press, 1981.

Steckenrider, Janie S., and Neal E. Cutler. "Aging and Adult Political Socialization: The Importance of Roles and Transitions." In *Political Learning in Adulthood: A Sourcebook of Theory and Research*, edited by Roberta S. Sigel. Chicago: University of Chicago Press, 1989.

Suedfeld, Peter, and Susan Bluck. "Changes in Integrative Complexity Accompanying Significant Life Events: Historical Evidence." *Journal of Personality and Social Psychology* 64 (1993): 124–130.

Tadmor, Carmit T., and Philip E. Tetlock. "Biculturalism: A Model of the Effects of Second-Culture Exposure on Acculturation and Integrative Complexity." *Journal of Cross-Cultural Psychology* 37 (2) (2006): 173–190.

Tetlock, Philip E. "A Value Pluralism Model of Ideological Reasoning. *Journal of Personality and Social Psychology* 50 (1986): 819–827.

Tetlock, Philip E. "The Impact of Accountability on Judgment and Choice: Toward a Social Contingency Model." *Advances in Experimental Social Psychology* 25 (1992): 331–376.

Thompson, Dennis. "Deliberative Democratic Theory and Empirical Political Science." *Annual Review of Political Science* 11 (2008): 497–520.

APPENDIX A:
METHODOLOGY

Selection of Class Cohort (CC)

To identify members of the class cohort to participate in the study, we used a random-number generator to select members of the WFU 2005 graduating class. While CC members were chosen at random, we wanted to match race/ethnicity, gender, and college major with the DF group as closely as possible. Therefore, these demographics were taken into account. We assembled a larger group of CCs (25) than DFs (20), in order to try to attain a close match, while also keeping selection of CC members random. The figures below compare the two groups based on the matching characteristics we used for the sample of 45 participants.

Figure A-1: Demographics for Preliminary Sample

Race/Ethnicity

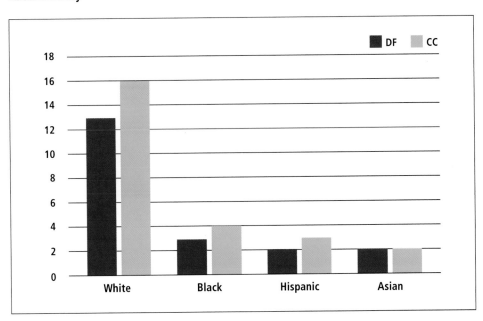

(Demographics continue on the next page.)

Gender

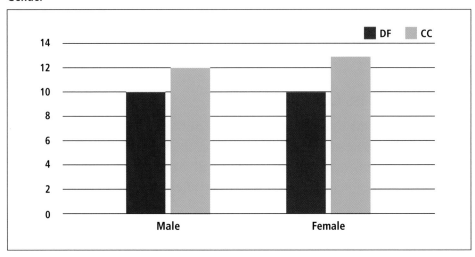

College Major

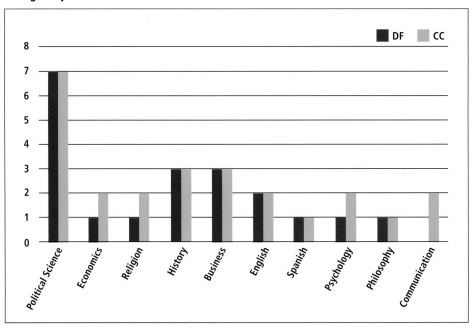

Research on selecting control groups in quasi-experimental designs like ours suggests that a good matching process can help to strengthen the ability to conclude that differences between the control and treatment groups were caused by the treatment rather than by other differences (Ho, et al. 2007). We felt it was important to aim for as close a demographic match as possible between the two groups in order to minimize the chances of arriving at flawed conclusions. This was done by reviewing the demographic categories that contained more CCs than DFs and randomly removing the extra CCs. Our final sample of 40 consisted of 20 DFs and 20 CCs, equally matched for college major and gender and closely matched for race/ethnicity. Figure A-2 below shows the demographics of our final sample.

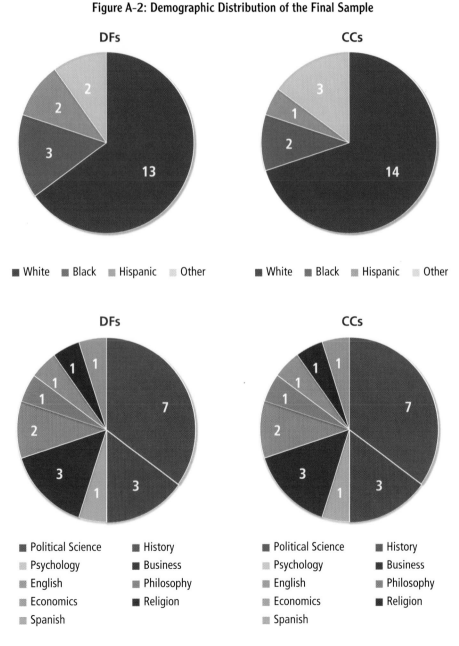

Figure A-2: Demographic Distribution of the Final Sample

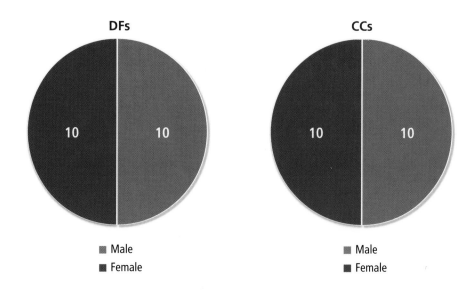

Instruments and Implementation

Interview and survey questions were constructed as follows:

1. We started with the findings from the 2001-2005 study and connected those findings to the particular interview questions and survey questions we used during that study.

2. We adapted those questions and added new ones, based on a review of the literature on the best ways of measuring political and civic engagement and attitudes about the political system, particularly those that have been tested and used with this age group (Bobek, et al. 2009; Delli Carpini and Keeter 1996; Flanagan, et al. 2007; Lopez, et al. 2006). Additional changes were made to reflect the fact that the subjects are no longer enrolled at Wake Forest and that, for the most part, their education is behind them.

We tested the interview and survey instruments with four young professionals who had graduated from college with bachelor's degrees in order to assess the average amount of time each would take to complete. As a result of the tests, we adjusted questions to keep the time within reasonable limits (1 hour for the phone interview; 20 minutes for the online survey) and made a few language changes to clarify the interview questions.

Between November 2013 and June 2014, we sent each of the participants a letter explaining the study and notifying them that our graduate research assistant would be contacting them to set up a phone interview. In order to avoid any interviewer bias in the DF interviews, all were conducted by our graduate assistant or by Christy Buchanan, who were not part of the original study. This allowed the DFs to critique the program, if they wished, without worrying about hurting the feelings of Professors Harriger and McMillan. The open-ended interview questions are shown in Appendix B. The use of Webex to conduct the interviews allowed "face-to-face" online communication, as well as recording of the interviews, which were then transcribed. A few participants did not have cameras on their computers, so only the audio portion of those interviews was recorded. Following completion of the phone interviews, participants filled out online surveys that asked questions about their political and civic participation activities (see Appendix C). We used the software program Qualtrics to conduct the survey. After completion of both the interview and survey, each participant received a $75 participation stipend.

ID numbers were assigned to participants as a way of eliminating direct identifiers. DFs were given an ID number beginning with the letter *D* followed by three digits beginning with the number *2*, and CCs were given an ID number beginning with the letter *C*, followed by three digits beginning with the number *1*. For the transcriptions that were used for analysis, we used these ID numbers to differentiate between DFs and CCs. All names and direct identifiers were removed from transcripts to help protect participants' confidentiality. Participants were asked to list their research ID numbers on the online surveys as well. This was also so that we would be able to differentiate DFs from CCs in the quantitative analyses and match online survey answers to interview answers, if desired. An additional step was added to reduce bias in quantitative coding and IC scoring. Specifically, all identifiers, including the participants' original ID numbers, were removed from transcripts for coding so that coders did not know whether the answers they were coding were from DFs or CCs. So we would eventually be able to match transcripts to the DF or CC group, new ID numbers were randomly created that were not indicative of which group the participant belonged to.

Content Analysis of Interview Data

To develop a coding system for answers to our open-ended interview questions, one or two members of our team first read through all the interviews to detect any themes that arose within sets of questions. They then proposed an initial set of codes for each group of questions, which were reviewed by the whole team. After making suggested changes, two team members used the codes on a subset of interviews to see whether there were any codes we needed to add, delete, or amend. Concerns were discussed with the entire team, if necessary. Once we felt confident in our codes, these two team members finalized the list.

All qualitative analyses were conducted through MAXQDA, a software program designed for qualitative coding and analyses. Interview questions were split into groups and different pairs of research team members were assigned to do the coding for each set of questions. Reliability was assessed based on inter-coder agreement. MAXQDA calculates inter-coder agreement using the following formula: % agreement = # of agreements / (# of agreements + # of non-agreements). For all questions, this reliability calculation was based on the codes from 20 interviews, which were coded by both coders. Reliability scores were as follows for each set of questions: preparation for civic and political life, 85.9%; definitions of citizenship and civic responsibilities, 91.5%; political involvement, 84.8%; changing politics, 98.5%; efficacy in community, work, and politics, 89.6%; political conversations and voice, 87.7%; sources of political information, 82.5%. Once reliability (over 80%) was obtained, the coders resolved differences on main constructs, and then each completed 10 interviews on their own.

Integrative Complexity Scoring (ICS)

In preparation for applying ICS to several of the questions from our interviews, we invited Mark Pancer, a recognized expert on ICS, to Wake Forest University to conduct a workshop on the method. The workshop was held April 9-10, 2014. In addition to teaching the methodology, Pancer also scored a sample of our data and we used his scores as a yardstick for practicing as a group on scoring our data. Once we were confident that we understood the method and had achieved reliability in the group, two trained graduate research assistants coded all of the data for the two questions concerning citizenship, which we used for the analysis. Katy Harriger also served as an outside coder who reviewed and checked answers that the primary coders were uncertain about. One of the graduate student coders had no knowledge of our hypotheses about potential differences between DFs and CCs. Inter-coder reliability for the two primary coders was .96.

Quantitative Analysis of Survey Data

Data collected through Qualtrics were downloaded into SPSS, checked, and cleaned. A codebook was created. Internal reliabilities (Cronbach's alpha) were computed for all known scales using our final sample of 40 participants. For scales with internal reliability greater than or equal to .70, scales were created by averaging items. For scales with lower internal reliabilities, we ran analyses at an item level rather than averaging the items and making our comparisons across these averages.

T-tests were used to compare mean differences between the DFs and CCs on items and scales. Due to our small sample size, for items and scales in which we had a prediction about directionality (e.g., we predicted that DFs would score higher than CCs) one-tailed t-tests were used in order to increase the power of our analyses.

Table A-1 provides the statistical data supporting Table 3 on page 52.

Table A-1: Significant Differences between Democracy Fellows (DF) and the Class Cohort (CC) on Survey Items

| | Group | | | |
	DF M (SD)	CC M (SD)	*t*	*df*
Read a newspaper for information on politics and current events	2.90 (1.07)	2.30 (1.03)	1.81*	38
People like me don't have a say about what the government does	2.00 (.86)	2.75 (1.29)	-2.16*	38
Running for office is an honorable thing to do	3.75 (.72)	3.25 (.97)	1.86*	38
I am in, or interested in, pursuing a career in politics and government	3.10 (1.41)	2.25 (1.33)	1.96*	38
Communicate with Others about Politics/Interest • I talk to other people about politics • I'm interested in other people's opinions about politics, even if those opinions are different from my views • I encourage others to express their opinions about politics, even if those opinions are different from my views • I enjoy talking about politics and political issues	3.98 (.91)	3.53 (.79)	1.67*	38
Degree to which your college education prepared you to serve your community	4.40 (.68)	3.85 (.99)	2.05**	38
Degree to which your college education prepared you to be active politically	4.10 (.79)	3.40 (1.14)	2.26**	38

Note. *p < .05. ** p < .001. M = Mean. SD = Standard Deviation.

APPENDIX B:
THE INTERVIEW INSTRUMENT

Interview Script and Questions

To all interviewees:

Hi, ...

I am (name/no title!!)...........and I'm a part of a team conducting a follow-up study begun with your class in 2001.

We would like to welcome you back, virtually, to your alma mater, and thank you for agreeing to participate in this study. Just for the record, could you please state your Research ID #.................. (if they cannot find it or are struggling, we can state it and ask them to confirm).

As you know from previous correspondence, the focus of this particular study is on young adults' social views and civic engagement. We hope to gather information from this interview and the subsequent online survey we have asked you to take within a week of the interview. This interview, of course, will be taped and transcribed, but strict confidentiality will be upheld, so that you may offer opinions and attitudes freely. If you feel uncomfortable about any of the questions, please just say so and we will move on, and of course, you are free to terminate the interview and your participation in the study if you choose.

We will be covering four general areas that we will identify as we go: (Tip to Interviewer: Repeat numbers since there is more than one concept in three of them.)

1) *Your views on CITIZENSHIP/POLITICS*

2) *Your perceptions of how much POWER and INFLUENCE you have*

3) *THE ROLE OF HIGHER EDUCATION IN CIVIC EDUCATION*

4) *THE SOURCES OF YOUR POLITICAL INFORMATION AND POLITICAL CONVERSATION*

5) *(* Only for Democracy Fellows *) Your experiences in the DEMOCRACY FELLOWS PROGRAM*

My role in this is to be the neutral interviewer—not to give much feedback or judge or manage your answers. There are no right or wrong answers to our questions, but if you need clarification on any of the questions, please ask.

First let's talk about your general thoughts and attitudes concerning CITIZENSHIP:

- What does it mean to you to be a citizen? What responsibilities of citizenship are required in your view?

- Has your definition of citizenship changed since you graduated from Wake Forest? If so, how?

- How involved in politics are you? What motivates you or stands in the way of political action? [Prompts: Job/work? Family? Continuing education? Free time?] Are there other things that tend to facilitate or impede your political involvement?

- Are you more, or less, equally involved in politics than you were in college? Why do you think that is?

- If you could change politics as it is currently practiced, what would you do?

Second, now I want to ask you some questions about your perceptions of your own POWER *or* INFLUENCE. *These questions may seem at first very similar to the things we just talked about, but there are some distinct differences in what we are trying to learn from you here.*

- First, I will ask you a series of questions concerning the degree to which you feel you have the ability to effect change in your current public life. First, to what degree do you feel you have the ability to effect change in your political environment? Your social/community life? Your professional environment/at your job? *(For each of these questions be sure to follow up as needed with how the interviewee perceives him/herself as a change agent, or does not).* Why do you think that is?

- Do you believe that you have more or less or the same amount of political power/influence that you felt you had when you graduated from college? Why might that be the case?

- Do you have as much political power/influence now as you anticipated when you graduated from college? Why do you think that is?

- How inclined are you to express an opinion on political or social issues? Why is that?

- Do you feel more or less or equally inclined to speak up or to otherwise express your opinion on political or social issues than you did when you graduated from college? Why?

Third, I'd like to ask you some questions about **THE ROLE OF HIGHER EDUCATION IN CIVIC EDUCATION.**

- Do you feel that your college education prepared you to serve your community? In what ways were you prepared? And in what ways were you not prepared?

- Do you feel that your college education prepared you to be politically active? Why or why not?

- In hindsight, can you recall where and in what form you received the most helpful civic preparation at Wake Forest? [Prompts if needed: class, student organizations, group discussions, service projects, informal conversations?]

- What advice do you have for Wake Forest as to the best way to prepare students for citizenship?

- In reflecting back more generally on your college years, what stands out to you about your experience at Wake Forest? (This can be about politics and civic engagement or about other things.)

- More generally, are there ways you can identify in which the Wake Forest experience has influenced your behavior or choices as a young adult?

We're going to move to the fourth topic area now. I want to ask you about **THE SOURCES OF YOUR POLITICAL INFORMATION AND CONVERSATION.**

- What are your primary sources of political information?

- Do you talk to anyone about politics? Count on anyone for information? Use anyone as a sounding board? If so, who are these people, and why have you chosen to talk to them? If not, why not?

- Have you engaged in structured dialogue or deliberation about social or political issues with other citizens in your community? Why or why not? If you have, did you find this experience worthwhile? Did you learn anything? Why or why not?

Before we close, I now want to ask you a few questions about American politics. These questions are a standard index used in polling research to measure political knowledge. Some of the questions may seem too easy or irrelevant but I hope you'll bear with me in answering them as this will help us align our research with national standards.

Knowledge Index Questions

(A standard measure reported in Delli Carpini and Keeter [1996, 304-306]).

- Do you happen to know what job or political office is now held by Joe Biden?

- Whose responsibility is it to determine if a law is constitutional or not? Is it the president, the Congress, or the Supreme Court?

- How much of a majority is required for the US Senate and House to override a presidential veto?

- Do you happen to know which party has the most members in the House of Representatives?

- Would you say that one of the parties is more conservative than the other at the national level? Which party is more conservative?

To the Democracy Fellows only :

Finally, we want to ask you some questions about your experiences in the Democracy Fellows program while you were at Wake Forest.

- In reflecting back on your participation in the Democracy Fellows program, what stands out about the experience?

- Are you finding any use for your deliberative experience in your post-college, adult life? If so, recall some examples. If not, why not?

- Are there other ways that the Democracy Fellows experience has influenced your behavior or choices?

Thank you so much for your time and your thoughts. We appreciate your help with this. Before we say goodbye, I just want to remind you that we will need you to answer the online survey during the next week. Shortly you should receive an e-mail from Stephanie, our graduate research assistant, with the link to this survey. Once you complete the survey she will contact you one more time to give you information on your compensation for taking part in this research study. Once again, thank you so much for your time!

APPENDIX C:
THE SURVEY INSTRUMENT

Thank you for taking the time to complete this survey. At times, some of the items may seem repetitive, but each question is asked for a reason and provides us with different information on young adults' social views and civic engagement.

ID (Please state the ID number you were given for your interview.)

1. Currently, how likely is it that you would do each of the following?

	Not at all Likely	Unlikely	Maybe	Likely	Extremely Likely
Contact or visit someone in government who represents your community					
Contact a newspaper, radio, or TV talk show to express your opinion on an issue					
Sign an e-mail or written petition					
Vote on a regular basis					
Wear a campaign button to support a candidate					
Volunteer for a political party					
Participate in a boycott against a company					
Refuse to buy products made under unfair labor conditions					
Participate in political activities, such as protests, marches, or demonstrations					
Do volunteer work for community organizations					

	Not at all Likely	Unlikely	Maybe	Likely	Extremely Likely
Get involved in issues like health or safety that affect your community					
Work with a group to solve a problem in the community where you live					
Run, walk, or bike to support a charity					
Raise money for a charity					

2. Indicate your current likelihood of giving financial support to one or more special interest groups (e.g., Greenpeace, NRA, PETA, AFL-CIO, the National Organization of Women, the American Civic Liberties Union).

   ☐ Not at all likely

   ☐ Unlikely

   ☐ Maybe

   ☐ Likely

   ☐ Extremely likely

3. Indicate your current likelihood of becoming involved in one or more special interest groups (e.g., Greenpeace, NRA, PETA, AFL-CIO, the National Organization of Women, the American Civic Liberties Union).

   ☐ Not at all likely

   ☐ Unlikely

   ☐ Maybe

   ☐ Likely

   ☐ Extremely likely

4. Using the following scale, indicate how important it is to you to:

	Not at all Likely	Unlikely	Maybe	Likely	Extremely Likely
...work to stop prejudice					
...improve race relations					
...help those who are less fortunate					
...help people in my community					
...do something to stop pollution					
...help protect animals					
...preserve the earth for future generations					
...serve my country in the military					
...be active in a religion					
...follow the principles of a religion					
...get a job where I won't get laid off					
...get a job that pays well					
...be active in politics					

5. The following questions ask about your participation in various activities. Have you ever done any of the following (Indicate "yes" or "no"):

	Yes	No
Signed an online petition		
Written an e-mail or letter advocating for a political position or opinion		
Attended a political rally or demonstration		
Contributed to an online discussion or blog advocating for a political position or opinion		

	Yes	No
Donated money to a political campaign or cause		
Volunteered on a political campaign for a candidate or an issue		
Liked a political issue on Facebook		
Liked a political candidate on Facebook		
Used your Facebook status to advocate for a political position		
Used Twitter to advocate for a political position		

6. Do you currently list a political view on your Facebook profile?

☐ Yes

☐ No

☐ Not Applicable

7. How much do you agree or disagree with each of these statements?

	Strongly Disagree	Disagree	Uncertain	Agree	Strongly Agree
I think people should assist those in their lives who are in need of help.					
I think it is important for people to follow rules and laws.					
I try to help when I see people in need.					
I am willing to help others without being paid.					
I try to be kind to other people.					
I think it is important to tell the truth.					
I work with others to change unjust laws.					
I think it is important to protest when something in society needs changing.					

	Strongly Disagree	Disagree	Uncertain	Agree	Strongly Agree
I think it is important to buy products from businesses that are careful not to harm the environment.					
I think it is important to challenge inequalities in society.					
Being actively involved in community issues is my responsibility.					
Being concerned about state and local issues is an important responsibility for everybody.					
I believe I can make a difference in my community.					
By working with others in the community I can help make things better.					

8. In a typical week, how often do you:

	Hardly at all	Only now and then	Some of the time	Most of the time
Watch the local news on TV for information on politics and current events				
Watch national news or cable shows (such as CNN) for information on politics and current events				
Listen to news about politics and current events on the radio				
Read a newspaper for information on politics and current events				
Read news on the Internet about politics and current events				

9. How much do you agree or disagree with each of these statements?

	Strongly Disagree	Disagree	Uncertain	Agree	Strongly Agree
I feel like I need more practical information about politics before I get involved.					
Elected officials seem to be motivated by selfish reasons.					
Politics is not relevant to my life right now.					
Political involvement rarely has any tangible results.					
It really doesn't matter to me who the president is.					
People like me don't have any say about what the government does.					
Running for office is an honorable thing to do.					
Community service is an honorable thing to do.					
Politics has become too partisan.					
The idea of working in some form of public service is appealing to me.					
I don't believe my vote will make a real difference.					
Politics today are no longer able to meet the challenges our country is facing.					
Elected officials don't seem to have the same priorities I have.					
Politics should be left to those who are interested in it.					
I am in, or interested in pursuing, a career in politics and government.					

10. **Have the results of your previous involvement in politics left you disappointed?**

- ☐ Yes
- ☐ No
- ☐ Not Applicable

11. **How much are each of the following like you?**

	Not at all like me	Not like me	Some like me	Like me	A lot like me
I listen to people talk about politics even when I know that I already disagree with them.					
When I see or read a news story about an issue, I try to figure out if they're just telling one side of the story.					
When I hear news about politics, I try to figure out what is REALLY going on.					

12. **The next set of questions asks for your opinion of elected officials (e.g., senators, members of city council, governor, president). Indicate how much you agree or disagree with each statement.**

	Strongly Disagree	Disagree	Uncertain	Agree	Strongly Agree
In general, elected officials cannot be trusted.					
Most elected officials listen to the citizens they represent.					
In general, elected officials give a lot of their time to make the community a better place.					
Generally, the only thing elected officials care about is money.					
In general, elected officials are concerned with serving their fellow citizens.					

13. The following questions ask about your opinions. Indicate how much you agree or disagree with each statement.

	Strongly Disagree	Disagree	Uncertain	Agree	Strongly Agree
Newspapers should not criticize the government.					
I support all US policies, no matter what.					
It is un-American to criticize the government.					
Basically, people get fair treatment in America, no matter who they are.					
In America you have an equal chance no matter where you come from or what race you are.					
America is a fair society where everyone has an equal chance to get ahead.					

14. To what extent would each of the following concerns motivate you to be politically involved?

	Not at All	A Little Bit	Somewhat	Quite a Lot	A Great Deal
I believe that it is important to reduce hunger and poverty in the world.					
I believe it is important to make the world a better place to live in.					
I believe it is important to make sure all people are treated fairly.					
I am concerned that everyone in America does not have the same rights and opportunities.					
When I think about the future, I worry that there will not be enough jobs to go around.					
I think it will be hard to make enough money to support a family.					

	Not at All	A Little Bit	Somewhat	Quite a Lot	A Great Deal
Economic changes in our country are making the life of the average person worse, not better.					
A few individuals are becoming richer but many people are becoming poorer.					
I worry that many people in my generation will not have steady jobs.					
I am concerned about how my tax dollars are used.					
I am concerned that my taxes are too high.					
My tax dollars are being used for things with which I disagree.					

15. The following questions ask about your opinions. Indicate how much you agree or disagree with each statement.

	Strongly Disagree	Disagree	Uncertain	Agree	Strongly Agree
I believe I can make a difference in my community.					
It's not really my problem if my neighbors are in trouble and need help.					
It is important for me to contribute to my community and society.					
When I see someone being taken advantage of, I want to help.					
I often think about doing things so that people in the future can have things better.					
When I see people being treated unfairly, I don't feel sorry for them.					

	Strongly Disagree	Disagree	Uncertain	Agree	Strongly Agree
I feel sorry for other people who don't have what I have.					
By working with others in the community, I can help make things better.					

16. Think about people in general. How much do you agree or disagree with the following statements?

	Strongly Disagree	Disagree	Uncertain	Agree	Strongly Agree
Most people can be trusted.					
Most people are fair and don't take advantage of you.					

17. How much do you agree or disagree with the following statements?

	Strongly Disagree	Disagree	Uncertain	Agree	Strongly Agree
I enjoy talking about politics and political issues.					
I talk to other people about politics.					
I'm interested in other people's opinions about politics, even if those opinions are different from my views.					
I encourage others to express their opinions about politics, even if those opinions are different from my views.					

18. Since graduating from college, have you done any of the following?

	Yes	No
Tried to talk to people and explain why they should vote for or against one of the parties or candidates during an election		
Expressed your views about politics on a website, blog, or chat room		

	Yes	No
Participated in a public discussion (face-to-face) where people expressed their views on a political or social issue		
Deliberated with members of your community about a public issue		
Worked as a canvasser (i.e., someone who goes door to door) for a political or social group, or candidate		

19. **Please answer the following questions about your college education:**

	Not at All	Very Little	Uncertain	Somewhat	A Great Deal
To what degree did your college education prepare you to serve your community?					
To what degree did your college education prepare you to be active politically?					

20. **If you found out about a problem in your community that you wanted to do something about (for example, illegal drugs were being sold near a school, or high levels of lead were discovered in the local drinking water), how well do you think you would be able to do each of the following?**

	I Definitely Can't	I Probably Can't	Maybe	I Probably Can	I Definitely Can
Create a plan to address the problem					
Get other people to care about the problem					
Organize and run a meeting					
Express your views in front of a group of people					
Identify individuals or groups who could help you with the problem					
Write an opinion letter to a local newspaper					

	I Definitely Can't	I Probably Can't	Maybe	I Probably Can	I Definitely Can
Call someone on the phone that you had never met before to get their help with the problem					
Contact an elected official about the problem					
Organize a petition					

21. In general, how comfortable are you doing each of the following:

	Very Uncomfort-able	Somewhat Uncomfort-able	Neutral	Somewhat Comfort-able	Very Comfort-able
Contacting a newspaper, radio, or TV talk show to express you opinion on an issue					
Contacting or visiting someone in government who represents your community					
Contacting an elected official about a problem					
Writing an opinion letter to a local newspaper					
Signing an e-mail or written petition that supports a view you hold					
Expressing your views in front of a group of people					

22. Which of the following statements best describes your voter registration status for the last presidential election held on November 6, 2012?

- ☐ I was registered
- ☐ I thought about registering, but didn't
- ☐ I tried to register, but was unable to
- ☐ I was not registered to vote on November 6
- ☐ Not sure

23. **Which of the following statements best describes your voting in the last presidential election held on November 6, 2012?**

☐ I voted at a polling place

☐ I voted early

☐ I voted absentee ballot

☐ I planned on voting, but wasn't able to

☐ I did not vote in this election

☐ I went to the polling place but wasn't allowed to vote

24. **Do you consider yourself to be politically engaged or politically active?**

☐ Yes

☐ No

25. **Please indicate how often you have participated in the following activities in the past 12 months:**

	Not at All	Less Than Once a Month	About Once a Month	A Few Times a Month	Weekly
Volunteered for community service					
Participated in a government, political, or issue-related organization					

26. **When it comes to voting, with which party do you consider yourself to be affiliated?**

☐ Strong Democrat

☐ Not a very strong Democrat

☐ Independent, leans Democrat

☐ Independent, does not lean either way

☐ Independent, leans Republican

☐ Not a very strong Republican

☐ Strong Republican

27. Among your closest friends, how many of them would you say share your political views?

☐ All of them

☐ Most of them

☐ Some of them

☐ None of them

☐ Don't know

28. Did your last/most recent significant other (e.g., girlfriend, boyfriend, or spouse) share your political beliefs?

☐ Yes

☐ No

☐ I don't know

☐ Not Applicable

29. When it comes to most political issues, do you think of yourself as a:

☐ Liberal

☐ Moderate leaning Liberal

☐ Moderate

☐ Moderate leaning Conservative

☐ Conservative

30. What is your gender?

☐ Male

☐ Female

31. What is your race and ethnicity?

☐ White, Non-Hispanic

☐ Black, Non-Hispanic

☐ Hispanic

☐ Other, Non-Hispanic

☐ Two or more races, Non-Hispanic

32. What is your current education level?

☐ Bachelor's degree

☐ Master's degree

☐ PhD

☐ Professional degree (MD, JD, MBA)

33. Which of the following describes your current marital status?

☐ Married

☐ Widowed

☐ Divorced

☐ Separated

☐ Remarried

☐ Never Married

☐ Living with Partner

34. How many children/stepchildren do you have?

35. Which of the following best describes your current employment status?

☐ Working as a paid employee

☐ Self-employed

☐ On temporary layoff from a job

☐ Looking for work

☐ Disabled

☐ Other, please explain _____

36. Which of the following best describes your occupation? (select all that apply)

☐ Military

☐ Education

☐ Transportation

☐ Law

☐ Politics

☐ Food Preparation and Serving
☐ Construction
☐ Office and Administration
☐ Sales
☐ Health and Human Services
☐ Business and Financial
☐ Computer and Mathematical
☐ Architecture and Engineering
☐ Student
☐ Other, please explain _____

37. **Are you a full-time or part-time student?**

☐ Full-time
☐ Part-time

38. **What degree are you pursuing?**

39. **What is your state of residence?**

40. **As an undergraduate at Wake Forest University, were you a part of the Democracy Fellows program?**

☐ Yes
☐ No